RADICAL
Forgiveness

D1026303

Making Room For the Miracle

By COLIN C. TIPPING

Radical Forgiveness, *Making Room for the Miracle*
First Printing: October 1997
Second Printing: June 1998
Third Printing, June 1999

Printed in the United States of America

Radical Forgiveness, Radical Forgiveness Therapy (RFT), and Satori Breathwork are Trademarks of Global 13 Company, Trust.

Library of Congress   97-074058
ISBN   1890412-03-1

Publisher:

Global 13 Publications Co., Trust
26 Briar Gate Lane, Marietta, GA 30066
Phone: (770) 428-9181
Fax: (770) 429-0276
E-mail *sales@radicalforgiveness.com*

Web Site: *www. radicalforgiveness.com*

Cover Design: Lightbourne Images
Editor: Nina Amir Lacey
Illustrations: JoAnna Tipping

Praise For This Book:

CAROLINE M. MYSS, Ph.D. — *author of "Anatomy of the Spirit," & "Why People Don't Heal and How They Can."*

"I LOVE this book! We can never say enough about the significance of forgiveness, nor offer people – including ourselves especially, enough guidance on how to accomplish this arduous task."

JOHN BRADSHAW — *PBS Broadcaster, lecturer, workshop leader and author of "Healing The Shame That Binds You," "Homecoming," "Creating Love" and "Family Secrets."*

"Anger work that does not take us towards forgiveness becomes just another addiction. This superb book gives us the tools that makes genuine forgiveness possible, enabling us to really move beyond our pain and heal our lives."

JEFF GATES — *author of "The Ownership Solution," and a consultant to U.S Government and governments worldwide.*

"The healing now needed in the world is not limited to individuals; it extends to nations, corporations and institutions. Yet the way forward has been blocked for the want of tools required for effective atonement, apology and forgiveness. Colin Tipping, a brilliant pioneer in this fast-emerging arena, provides just the sort of transformational tools required if we are to leave for our children a more peaceful and harmonious world."

CANDACE APPLE — *Owner of The Phoenix & Dragon Bookstore, Atlanta, GA,*

"People are buying this book for themselves and then coming back to buy many more for their friends. This is precisely the word-of-mouth phenomena that launched Celestine Prophecy and Conversations With God. I have learned through my ten years of bookselling that this is a certain predictor of a best seller."

CATHERINE PONDER — *Unity Church Worldwide. Author of "The Dynamic Laws of Prosperity" The Dynamic Laws of Healing."*

"I receive so many requests to endorse books that I have a "no endorsement" policy. But this one on forgiveness is so needed, that I am making an exception in this case. My readers write me of the most amazing experiences they have from practicing the miracle power of forgiveness. Try forgiveness for yourself and feel the relief; then make way for whatever miracles you need next in your life. This book shows you how!"

BRAD STEIGER — *author of "One With the Light" and "The Healing Power of Love."*

"Colin Tipping challenges us to practice "Radical Forgiveness," in order to accomplish truly dramatic healing and transformation in our own lives and in the lives of those with whom we interact. He sets all this out in a readily accessible, step-by-step process and provides us with the necessary tools to achieve the goal of true, rather than superficial, forgiveness."

JOHN HARRICHARAN — *award winning author of "When You Can Walk on Water, Take the Boat."*

"Colin Tipping's Radical Forgiveness is a remarkable guide for living. The reader quickly discovers how to move from victim to victor – from fear to freedom. This book is a MUST read for everyone for it will change the way you feel about the past while, at the same time, empowering you to create a magnificent future."

ALAN COHEN — *best selling author of "The Dragon Doesn't Live Here Any More," and "I Had It All the Time."*

"The book is magnificent and I am proud to endorse it wholeheartedly. Radical Forgiveness is a masterfully presented system of undoing what has caused pain in people's lives. My hat's off to Colin Tipping for joining heart and mind to bring illumination to a most important area. Practice these dynamic principles and your life will become new!"

Dedicated to the memory of
Diana, Princess of Wales

"Goodbye England's Rose"
(Epilogue, page 251)

Acknowledgements

My gratitude and love goes first to my wife, JoAnna, for believing in me and giving me total support for writing this book, even when times got hard. I also owe a great debt of gratitude to my sister Jill, and brother-in-law, Jeff, for allowing me to publish a very personal story about them both, without which this book would have been very much impoverished. I also acknowledge Jeff's daughter Lorraine and my daughter Lorraine for the same reason and all the members of Jill's and Jeff's family who were willing to read the book and to see the best in each person who had a part to play in Jill's story. I also acknowledge my brother John who witnessed the unfolding of the story, for his patience and support. I owe a special debt of gratitude to Michael Ryce for his inspiration on the forgiveness worksheets and to Arnold Patent for introducing me to spiritual law. Thanks are due to Nina Lacey for her careful editing and reviewing and to Lana Weber for her proof-reading and suggestions for last minute improvements. Then there are many others who have contributed to the process in all sorts of different but important ways and given support for which I shall always be grateful. My dear friend Lucie Pennewill, Burge Smith, Pamela Black, David Crawford, Andrea Hopke, Steve Grable, Pete Allen, Karen Hodges, Trisha McCannon, George Poirier, Dennis McCauley, Jean Smith, Farra Allen, Gregory Possman, Sandy Bellamy, Fahy Van-Putten, Laurie Lacy, Robyn Stalson, Joseph & Katherine Whitner, Vinita Watkins, Ted & Mary Macy, Barbara Roberts, Rick & Jeni Prigmore, Kathie Lumberg, John Harricharan, Anita Bergen, Jeannette Slygh, Rick Neal, Tom Cabannis, Ann McElfresh, Dell Dorenbosch, Jay Finnerty, Carole O'Connell and Unity North Church, Donna Gates, and many, many more. Finally, my love and gratitude to my mother and my father for choosing to have me and for accepting my request to incarnate through them.

Contents

ILLUSTRATIONS & TABLES

Introduction

Everywhere we look — in the newspapers, TV, and even in our own personal lives, we see examples of egregiously hurt victims. We read, for example, that at least one out of every five adults in America today was either physically or sexually abused as a child. TV news confirms that rape and murder is commonplace in our communities and crime against the person and property is rampant everywhere. Around the world we see torture, repression, incarceration, genocide and open warfare occurring on a vast scale.

Over a period of ten years, since I began doing forgiveness workshops, cancer retreats and corporate seminars, I have heard enough horror stories from quite ordinary people to convince me that there is not a human being on the planet that has not been seriously victimized at least once in their lifetime, and in minor ways more times than they could count. Who among us could say they have never blamed someone else for their lack of happiness? For most, if not all of us, that simply is a way of life.

Indeed, the victim archetype is deeply engrained in all of us, and exerts great power in the mass consciousness. For eons we have been playing out victimhood in every aspect of our lives, convincing ourselves that victim consciousness is absolutely fundamental to the human condition.

The time has come to ask ourselves the question — how can we stop creating our lives this way and let go of the victim archetype as the model of how to live our lives?

To break free from such a powerful archetype, we must replace it with something *radically* different — something so compelling and spiritually liberating that it magnetizes us away from the victim archetype and the world of illusion. We need something that will take us beyond the drama of our lives so we can see the big picture and the *truth* that, right now, lies hidden from us. When we awaken to that truth, we will understand the true meaning of our suffering and be able to transform it immediately.

As we move into the new millenium and the Aquarian Age (see page 68), and prepare for the imminent next great leap in our spiritual evolution, it is essential that we adopt a way of living based not on fear, control and abuse of power, but on true forgiveness, unconditional love and peace. That's what I mean by something *radical*, and that is what my book is all about — helping us make that transition. That is my commitment.

To transform anything, we must be able to experience it completely and fully, which means that to transform the victim archetype, we must experience victimhood fully. There is no short cut! Therefore, we need situations in our lives that allow us to feel victimized so we can transform the energy through **Radical Forgiveness.**

To transform an energy pattern so fundamental as the victim archetype, many, many souls must accept this as their spiritual mission — souls who possess the wisdom and love necessary to accomplish this immense task. Perhaps you are one of the souls who volunteered for this mission. Could that be why this book speaks to you?

Jesus gave a powerful demonstration of what transforming the victim archetype means and I believe he now waits patiently and lovingly for us to follow his lead. Up to now at least, we have failed to learn from his example precisely because the victim archetype has had such a strong hold in our psyche.

We have ignored the lesson of genuine forgiveness that Jesus taught by straddling the fence and attempting to forgive while staying committed to being a victim. We have even turned Jesus into the ultimate victim. This will not move us forward in our spiritual evolution. True forgiveness must include letting go of victim consciousness.

Indeed, my main intention in writing this book was to make clear the distinction between forgiveness that maintains the victim archetype and **Radical Forgiveness** that frees us from it. Radical Forgiveness challenges us to radically shift our perception of the world and our interpretations of what happens to us in our lives so we can stop being a victim. My one goal is to help you make that shift.

I recognize that the ideas I am presenting here might be extremely challenging for someone severely victimized and still carrying a lot of pain. I ask only that you read with an open mind and see whether or not you feel better after reading it.

I write this revised introduction as I go into the second printing of the book and I can only tell you that the feedback I have been getting from my readers and from those who come to my workshops is overwhelmingly positive.

Even people who have been in emotional pain for a long time have found the book to be extremely freeing and healing — and the workshops transformational.

What has also been amazing and gratifying is the extent to which Chapter One, *'Jill's Story,'* has created instant healing for many, many people. I originally thought I was writing it as a useful lead-in to the concepts and ideas about Radical Forgiveness, but I now recognize that Spirit knew better and was guiding my hand all the way on this. I get many phone calls from people, often still in tears, who, having just read the story, tell me that they see themselves in it and feel that their healing has already begun.

A great many of these have been moved to share their experience with others by E-mailing *'Jill's Story'* directly from my web site* to all their friends, relations and business associates — a wonderful chain reaction!

I shall be forever grateful to my sister and brother-in-law for allowing me to tell their story and for making that gift to the world.

I find myself very humbled by the overall response I am getting to the book and it is fast becoming clear to me that I am being used by Spirit to get this message out so that we can all heal, raise our vibration and go home. I am grateful to be of service.

Namaste

Colin Tipping   Atlanta, GA.   July 1998
                                 * *www.radicalforgiveness.com*

PART ONE
A Radical Healing

Author's Note

*T*o *give you, the reader, an understanding of what I call Radical Forgiveness, I have presented the following true account of how this process saved my sister's marriage and changed her life. Since that time, Radical Forgiveness has positively impacted the lives of countless others, for, not long after this episode with my sister, I realized that the process she experienced could be used as a form of therapy quite different from any normal psychotherapy or common relationship counseling. Subsequently, I have offered Radical Forgiveness Therapy (RFT) to clients in my private practice and have used it with people in my workshops. I also offer training and certification in RFT (See Appendix 1.) I seldom need to use any other tool now, since I find that most so-called problems can be resolved with RFT.*

C.T.

1: Jill's Story

As soon as I saw my sister, Jill, emerge into the lobby of Atlanta's Hartsfield International Airport, I knew something was wrong. She had never hidden her feelings well, and it was apparent to me that she was in emotional pain.

Jill had flown from England to the United States with my brother John, whom I had not seen for sixteen years. He emigrated from England to Australia in 1972 and I to America in 1984 — thus Jill was, and still is, the only one of the three siblings living in England. John had made a trip home, and this trip to Atlanta represented the last leg of his return journey. Jill accompanied him to Atlanta so she could visit me and my wife, JoAnna, for a couple of weeks and see him off to Australia from there.

After the initial hugging and kissing and a certain amount of awkwardness, we set out for the hotel. I had arranged rooms for one night so JoAnna and I could show them Atlanta the next day before driving north to our home.

As soon as the first opportunity for serious discussion presented itself, Jill said, "Colin, things are not good at home. Jeff and I might be splitting up."

Despite the fact that I had noticed something seemed wrong with my sister, this announcement surprised me. I had always thought she and her husband, Jeff, were happy in their six-year-old marriage. Both had been married before, but this relationship had seemed strong. Jeff had three kids with his previous wife, while Jill had four. Her youngest son, Paul, was the only one still living at home.

"What's going on?" I asked.

"Well, it's all quite bizarre, and I don't quite know where to begin," she replied, "but Jeff is acting really strange, and I can't stand much more of it. We've gotten to the point where we can't talk to each other any more, and it's killing me. He has totally turned away from me and says that it's all my fault."

"Tell me about it," I said, flipping a glance at John, who responded by rolling his eyes. He'd stayed at their house for a week prior to flying to Atlanta, and I guessed by his demeanor that he'd heard enough of this subject to last him a while.

"Do you remember Jeff's eldest daughter, Lorraine?" Jill asked. I nodded. "Well, her husband got killed in a car crash about a year ago. Ever since then, she and Jeff have developed this really weird relationship. Any time she calls, he fawns over her, calling her *'Love,'* and spending hours talking to her in hushed tones. You'd think they were lovers — not father and daughter. If he's in the middle of something and she calls, he drops everything to talk with her. If she comes to our home, he acts just the same — if not worse. They huddle together in this deep and hushed conversation that excludes everyone else — especially me. I can hardly stand it. I feel she has become the center of his life, and I hardly figure in at all. I feel totally shut out and ignored."

She went on and on, offering more details of the strange family dynamic that had developed. JoAnna and I listened attentively. We wondered aloud about the cause of Jeff's behavior and were generally sympathetic. We made suggestions as to how she might talk to him about his behavior and generally struggled to find a way to fix things, as would any concerned brother and sister-in-law. John was supportive and offered his perspective on the situation as well.

What seemed strange and suspicious to me was the uncharacteristic nature of Jeff's behavior. The Jeff I knew was affectionate with his daughters and certainly co-dependent enough to badly need their approval and love, but I had never seen him behave in the manner Jill described. I had always known him as caring and affectionate towards Jill. In fact, I found it hard to believe that he would treat her quite so cruelly. I found it easy to understand why this situation made Jill unhappy, and Jeff's insistence that she was imagining it all and making herself mentally ill over it, only made matters worse for her.

The conversation continued all the next day. I began to get a picture of what might be going on between Jill and Jeff from a Radical Forgiveness standpoint, but decided

9

not to mention it — at least not right away. She was too caught up in the drama of the situation and wouldn't have been able to listen to what I had to say. Besides, Radical Forgiveness is based on metaphysical principles, and I had never had an opportunity to discuss metaphysics with either John or Jill. As far as I knew, neither had any knowledge of esoteric thought or metaphysical systems, and I felt certain that they were unaware of my beliefs about Radical Forgiveness. I felt the time had not yet arrived to introduce so challenging a thought as *this is perfect just the way it is — and an opportunity to heal.*

However, after the second day of verbally going round and round about the problem, I decided the time was near for me to try the Radical Forgiveness approach. This would require that my sister open up to the possibility that something beyond the obvious was happening — something that was purposeful, divinely guided and intended for her highest good. Yet, she was so committed to being the *victim* in the situation, I wasn't sure I could get her to hear an interpretation of Jeff's behavior that would take her out of that role.

However, just as my sister began yet another repetition of what she had said the day before, I decided to intervene. Tentatively, I said, "Jill, are you willing to looking at this situation differently? Would you consider letting go of how you are thinking for just a few hours and trying on a completely different way of looking at this situation?"

She looked at me quizzically, as if she were wondering,

'How can there possibly be another interpretation? It is how it is!' However, I have a certain track record with Jill in that I had helped her solve a relationship problem before, so she trusted me enough to say, "Well, I guess so. What do you have in mind?"

This was the opening I was waiting for. "What I'm going to say may sound strange, but try not to question it until I have finished. Just stay open to the possibility that what I am saying is true, and see whether or not what I say makes sense to you in any way at all."

Until this time, John had done his best to stay attentive to Jill, but the constant repetitive conversation about Jeff had begun to bore him tremendously. In fact, he had largely tuned her out. However, I was acutely aware that my interjection caused John to perk up and begin listening again.

"What you have described to us, Jill, certainly represents the truth as you see it," I began. "I have not the slightest doubt about the veracity of everything you have said. In case you ever doubted your own memory, as well you might have given Jeff's tendency to tell you that the whole situation is all in your mind, John has also witnessed much of the situation over the last three weeks and confirms your story, right John?" I queried, turning toward my brother.

"Absolutely," he confirmed. "I saw it going on a lot, just as Jill says. I thought it was pretty strange and, quite honestly, much of the time I felt awkward being there."

"I'm not surprised," I said. "Anyway Jill, I want you to know that nothing I am going to say negates what you have said or invalidates your story. I believe that it happened the way you said it happened. Let me, however, give you a hint of what might be going on underneath this situation."

"What do you mean, *underneath the situation*," Jill asked, eyeing me suspiciously.

"It's perfectly natural to think that everything *out there* is *all* there is to reality," I explained, "but maybe there's a whole lot more happening beneath that reality. We don't perceive anything else going on because our five senses are inadequate to the task. But that doesn't mean it isn't occurring.

"Take your situation. You and Jeff have this drama going on. That much is clear. What if, beneath the drama, something of a more spiritual nature was happening — same people and same events — but a totally different meaning? What if your two souls were doing the same dance but to a wholly different tune? What if the dance was about you healing? What if you could see this as an opportunity to heal and grow? That would be a very different interpretation, would it not?"

Both she and John looked at me as if I were now speaking a foreign language. I decided to back off from the explanation and to go directly for the experience.

"Looking back over the last three months or so Jill," I went on, "What did you feel mostly when you saw Jeff behaving so lovingly towards his daughter, Lorraine?"

"Anger mostly," she said, but continued thinking about it. "Frustration," she added — then, after a long pause, "And sadness. I really feel sad." Tears welled up in her eyes. "I feel so alone and unloved," she said and began sobbing quietly. "It wouldn't be so bad if I thought he couldn't show love, but he can and he does — but with *her!*"

She spat the last few words out with vehemence and rage and began to sob uncontrollably for the first time since her arrival. She'd shed a few tears prior to this, but she hadn't really let herself cry. Now, at last, she was letting go. I was pleased that Jill had been able to get in touch with her emotions that quickly.

A full 10 minutes went by before her crying subsided and I felt she could talk. At that point, I asked, "Jill, can you ever remember feeling this same way when you were a little girl?" Without the slightest hesitation, she said, "Yes." She was not immediately forthcoming about when, so I asked her to explain. It took her a while to respond.

"Dad wouldn't love me either!" she blurted out finally and began to sob again. "I wanted him to love me, but he wouldn't. I thought he couldn't love anyone! Then your daughter came along, Colin. He loved her all right. So why couldn't he love me, God damnit!" She banged her fist hard on the table as she shouted the words and dissolved into more uncontrollable tears.

13

Jill's reference was to my eldest daughter, Lorraine. Coincidentally, or rather, synchronistically, she and Jeff's eldest daughter had the same name.

Crying felt good to Jill. Her tears served as a powerful release and possibly a turning point for her. A real breakthrough might not be far away, I thought.

"Tell me about the incident with my daughter, Lorraine, and Dad." I said.

"Well," Jill said, while composing herself. "I always felt unloved by Dad and really craved his love. He never held my hand, or sat me on his lap much. I always felt there must be something wrong with me. When I was older, Mom told me she didn't think Dad was capable of loving anyone, not even her. At that time, I, more or less, made peace with that. I rationalized that if he wasn't really capable of loving anyone, then it wasn't my fault that he didn't love me. He really didn't love anyone. He hardly ever made a fuss of my kids — his own grandchildren — much less people or kids not his own. He was not a bad father. He just couldn't love. I felt sorry for him."

She cried some more, taking her time now. I knew what she meant about our father. He was a kind and gentle man but very quiet and withdrawn. For the most part, he certainly had seemed emotionally unavailable to anyone.

As Jill became more composed once again, she continued. "I remember a particular day at your house. Your daughter

Lorraine was probably about four or five years old. Mom and Dad were visiting from Leicester, and we all came to your house. I saw your Lorraine, take Dad's hand. She said, *'Come on, Grandad. Let me show you the garden and all my flowers.'* He was like putty in her hands. She led him everywhere and talked and talked and talked, showing him all the flowers. She enchanted him. I watched them out of the window the whole time. When they came back in, he put her on his lap and was as playful and joyful as I have ever seen him.

"I was devastated. *'So, he is able to love after all,'* I thought. If he could love Lorraine, then why not me?" The last few words came out as a whisper followed by deep long tears of grief and sadness, tears held in for all those years.

I figured we had done enough for the time being, and suggested we make tea. *(Well, we're English! We always make tea, no matter what!)*

Interpreting Jill's story from a Radical Forgiveness standpoint, I easily saw that Jeff's outwardly strange behavior was unconsciously designed to support Jill in healing her unresolved relationship with her father. If she could see this and recognize the perfection in Jeff's behavior, she could heal her pain — and Jeff's behavior would almost certainly stop. However, I wasn't sure how to explain this to Jill in a way she could understand at this point in time. Luckily, I didn't have to try. She stumbled on the obvious connection by herself.

15

Later that day she asked me, "Colin, don't you think it's odd that Jeff's daughter and your daughter both have the same name? Come to think of it, both of them are blonde and first born. Isn't that a strange coincidence! Do you think there's a connection?"

I laughed, and replied, "Absolutely. It's the key to understanding this whole situation."

She looked at me long and hard. "What do you mean?"

"Work it out for yourself," I replied. "What other similarities do you see between that situation with Dad and my Lorraine, and your current situation?"

"Well, let's see," said Jill. "Both girls have the same name. Both of them were getting what I don't seem to be able to get from the men in my life."

"What?" I enquired.

"Love," she said in a whisper.

"Go on," I urged gently.

"It seems that your Lorraine, was able to get the love from Dad that I couldn't. And Jeff's daughter, Lorraine, gets all the love she wants from her Dad, but at my expense. Oh, my God!" she exclaimed. She really was beginning to understand now.

"But why? I don't understand why. It's a bit frightening! What the hell's going on?" she asked in a panic.

It was time to put the pieces together for her. "Look, Jill," I said. "Let me explain how this works. This happens to be a perfect example of what I was talking about earlier when I said that beneath the drama we call life lies a whole different reality. Believe me, there's nothing to be frightened about. When you see how this works, you will feel more trust, more security and more peace than you ever thought possible. You'll realize how well we are being supported by the Universe or God, whatever you want to call it, every moment of every day no matter how bad any given situation seems at the time." I said as reassuringly as I could.

"Seen from a spiritual standpoint, our pain and discomfort in any given situation provides a signal that we are out of alignment with spiritual law and are being given an opportunity to heal something. This may be some original pain or perhaps a toxic belief that stops us from becoming our true selves. We don't often see it from this perspective, however. Rather, we judge the situation and blame others for what is happening, which prevents us from seeing the message or understanding the lesson. This prevents us from healing. If we don't heal whatever needs to be healed, we must create more discomfort until we are literally forced to ask, *'What is going on here?'* Sometimes the message has to become very loud, or the pain extremely intense, before we pay attention. A life threatening illness, for example, provides a loud message. Yet, even when facing death some people don't get the connection between what

17

is happening in their lives and the opportunity for healing that it provides.

"In your case, what has come up to be healed this time is your original pain around your father and the fact that he never showed you love. That is what all your current pain and discomfort is about. This particular pain has arisen many times before in different situations, but, because you didn't recognize the opportunity, it never got healed. That's why having yet another opportunity to look at and heal this issue is a gift!"

"A gift?" Jill questioned. "You mean it's a gift because there's a message in it for me? One that I might have gotten a long time ago if I'd been able to see it?"

"Yes," I said. "Had you seen it then, your discomfort would have been less and you wouldn't be going through this now. No matter. Now is fine, too. This is perfect, and you won't now have to produce a life-threatening illness to understand this, like so many people do. You're getting it now; you're beginning to understand and to heal.

"Let me explain to you exactly what happened and how it has effected your life up until now," I said, wanting her to understand clearly the dynamics of her current situation.

"As a little girl, you felt abandoned and unloved by Dad. For a girl, this is devastating. From a developmental standpoint, it is necessary for a young girl to feel loved by her father. Since you didn't feel that love, you concluded that there must something wrong with you. You began to really believe you were unlovable and inherently *not enough*. That belief anchored itself deeply in your subconscious mind and, later, when it came to relationships, began to run your life. In other words, as a way of mirroring your subconscious belief that you were *not enough*, your life always has included actual situations exhibiting to you the fact that you were, indeed, not enough. Life will always prove your beliefs right.

"As a child, the pain of not getting Dad's love was more than you could bear, so you suppressed some of the pain and repressed a whole lot more. When you suppress emotion, you know its there, but you stuff it down. Repressed emotion, on the other hand, gets buried so deeply in the subconscious mind that you lose awareness of it.

"Later, when you began to realize that your father was not a naturally loving man and probably couldn't love anyone, you began to somewhat rehabilitate or heal yourself from the affects of feeling unloved by him. You probably released some of the suppressed pain and maybe began to give up some part of the belief that you were unlovable. After all, if he couldn't love anyone, maybe it wasn't your fault after all that he didn't love you.

"Then, along comes the bombshell that knocked you right back to square one. When you observed him loving my Lorraine, that triggered your original belief. You said to yourself, *'My father can love after all, but he doesn't love me. It is obviously my fault. I am not enough for my father, and I will never be enough for any man.'*

19

From that point on, you continually created situations in your life to support your belief that you are *not enough.*"

"How have I done that?" Jill interrupted. "I don't see how I have created myself not being enough in my life."

"How was your relationship with Henry, your first husband?" I responded. She had been married to Henry, the father of her four children, for 15 years.

"Not bad in many respects, but he was so unfaithful. He was always looking for opportunities to have sex with other women, and I really hated that."

"Exactly. And, you saw him as the villain and you as the victim in that situation. However, the truth is, you attracted him into your life precisely because, at some level, you knew he would prove your belief about not being enough. By being unfaithful, he would support you in being right about yourself."

"Are you trying to say he was doing me a favor? I sure as hell don't buy that!" she said laughingly, but also with some not-too-well-disguised anger.

"Well, he certainly supported your belief, didn't he?" I replied. "You were so *not enough* that he always was on the lookout for other women, for *something more*. If he had done the opposite and consistently treated you as if you were totally enough by being faithful, you would have created some other drama in your life to prove your belief.

Your belief about yourself, albeit a totally false one, made it impossible for you to be enough.

"By the same token, had you at that time changed your belief by healing your original pain around your father and changed your belief to *I am enough*, Henry would have immediately stopped propositioning your friends. If he hadn't, you would have felt perfectly happy to leave him and find someone else who would treat you as though you were enough. We always create our reality according to our beliefs. If you want to know what your beliefs are, look at what you have in your life. Life always reflects our beliefs."

Jill seemed a bit perplexed, so I decided to reiterate some of the points I had made. "Each time Henry cheated on you, he gave you the opportunity to heal your original pain around being unloved by Dad. He demonstrated, and acted out for you, your belief that you were never going to be enough for any man. The first few times this happened, you may have gotten so mad and upset that you could have gotten in touch with the original pain and become acquainted with your belief system about yourself. In fact, his first acts of unfaithfulness represented your first opportunities to practice Radical Forgiveness and to heal your original pain, but you missed them. You made him wrong each time and created yourself as a victim instead, which made healing impossible."

"What do you mean forgiveness," Jill asked, still looking troubled. "Are you saying I should have forgiven him for screwing my best friend and anyone else who was willing?"

21

"I am saying that, at that time, he provided you with an opportunity to get in touch with your original pain and to see how a certain belief about yourself was running your life. In so doing, he gave you the opportunity to understand and change your belief, thus healing your original pain. That's what I mean by forgiveness. Can you see that, Jill?"

"Yes, I think so," she said. "He was reflecting my belief — the one I had formed because I felt so unloved by Dad. He was making me right about not being enough. Is that correct?"

"Yes, and to the extent that he provided you with that opportunity, he deserves credit — actually, more than you realize right now. We have no way of knowing whether he would have stopped his behavior had you healed your issue around Dad at that time — or whether you would have left him. Either way, he would have served you powerfully well. So, in that sense, he deserves not only your forgiveness but your deep gratitude as well. And you know what? It wasn't his fault that you didn't understand the true message behind his behavior.

"I know that it was, and may still be, hard for you to see that he was trying to give you a great gift. That's not how we are taught to think. We're not taught to look at what is going on in our lives and to say, *'Look what I have created in my life? Isn't that interesting.'* Instead, we are taught to judge, lay blame, accuse, play victim and seek revenge.

Neither are we taught to think that our lives are directed by forces other than our own conscious mind — but, in truth, they are.

"In fact, it was Henry's *soul* that tried to help you heal. On the surface, Henry just acted out his sexual addiction, but his soul — working with your soul — chose to use the addiction for your spiritual growth. Recognizing this fact is what Radical Forgiveness is all about. Its purpose lies in seeing the truth behind the apparent circumstances of a situation and recognizing the love that always exists there."

I felt that talking about her current situation would help Jill fully understand the principles I had described. So, I said, "Let's take another look at Jeff and see how these principles are operating in your current relationship. In the beginning, Jeff was extremely loving towards you. He really doted on you, did things for you, communicated with you. On the surface, life with Jeff seemed pretty good.

"Remember, though, this didn't fit your picture of yourself — your belief about yourself. According to your belief, you shouldn't have a man who shows you this much love. You are not enough, remember?"

Jill nodded, but still looked uncertain and rather perplexed.

"Your soul knows you must heal that belief, so it colludes with Jeff's soul somehow to bring it to your awareness. On the surface it seems that Jeff begins to act strangely and totally out of character. He then taunts you by loving

23

another Lorraine, thus acting out with you the very same scenario you had with your father many years ago. He appears to be persecuting you mercilessly, and you feel totally helpless and victimized. Does this describe, more or less, you current situation?" I asked.

"I guess so," Jill said quietly. She wrinkled her brow as she tried to hold on to the new picture of her situation slowly forming in her mind.

"Well, here you are again, Jill, about to make a choice. You must choose whether to heal and to grow — or to be right," I said and smiled.

"If you make the choice people normally make, you will choose to be the victim and make Jeff wrong, which, in turn, allows you to be right. After all, his behavior seems quite cruel and unreasonable, and I doubt there are many women who wouldn't support you in taking some drastic action in response to it. Haven't most of your friends been saying you should leave him?"

"Yes," she replied. "Everyone says I should get out of the marriage if he doesn't change. I actually thought that you would say that too," she said with a tinge of disappointment.

"A few years ago, I probably would have," I said and laughed. "However, since my introduction to these spiritual principles, my whole way of looking at such situations has changed, as you can see," I said with a wry smile, looking across at John. He grinned, but said nothing.

I continued. "So, as you might guess, the other choice might be to recognize that what seems to be happening on the surface is just an illusion and that something else much more meaningful — and potentially healing — is going on. You can accept that Jeff's behavior may possess another message, another meaning, another intent, and that within the situation lies a gift for you."

Jill thought for a while, then said, "Jeff's behavior is so damn bizarre you'd have a hard time coming up with any good reason for it. Maybe something else is going on that I don't yet see. I suppose its similar to what Henry was doing, but it's hard for me to see it with Jeff, because I 'm so confused right now. I can't see beyond what actually is going on."

"That's okay," I said reassuringly. "Look, there's no need to figure it out. Just being willing to entertain the idea that something else is going on is a giant step forward. In fact, the willingness to see the situation differently is the key to your healing. 90% of the healing occurs when you become willing to let in the idea that your soul has lovingly created this situation for you. In becoming willing, you let go of control and surrender it to God. He takes care of the other 10%. If you can really understand at a deep level and surrender to the idea that God will handle this for you if you turn it over to him, you won't need to do anything at all. The situation and your healing will both get handled automatically."

"However, prior even to this step, you can take a perfectly rational step that enables you to see things differently right away. It involves separating fact from fiction. It means recognizing that your belief has no factual basis whatsoever. It is simply a story you have made up, based on a few facts and a whole lot of interpretation.

We do this all the time. We experience an event and make interpretations about it. Then, we put these two pieces together to create a largely false story about what happened. The story becomes the belief, and we defend it as if it were the truth. It never is, of course.

"In your case, the facts were that Dad didn't hug you, didn't spend time playing with you, didn't hold you, didn't put you on his lap. He did not meet your needs for affection. Those were the facts. On the basis of those facts, you made a crucial assumption: *'Dad doesn't love me.'* Isn't that true?" She nodded.

"However, the fact that he didn't meet your needs doesn't mean that he didn't love you. That's an interpretation. It probably wasn't true. He was a sexually repressed man and intimacy was scary for him; we know that about him. Maybe he just didn't know how to express his love in the way you wanted to receive it. Do you remember that super doll's house he made you one year for Christmas? I remember him spending countless hours on it in the evenings. Perhaps that was the only way he knew how to express his love for you.

"I'm not making excuses for him or trying to make what

you have said, or felt, wrong. I'm just trying to point out how we all make the mistake of thinking that our interpretations represent the truth."

"The next big assumption you made," I continued, "based on the facts *and* your first interpretation that *'Dad doesn't love me,'* was *'It's my fault. There must be something wrong with me.'* That was an even greater lie than the other assumption, don't you agree?" She nodded.

"It isn't surprising that you would come to that conclusion, because that's the way little kids think. Since they perceive that the world revolves around them, they always assume that when things don't go well, it's their fault. When a child first thinks this, the thought is coupled with great pain. To reduce the pain, a child represses it, but this action actually makes it all the harder to get rid of the thought. Thus, we stay stuck with the idea *'it's my fault and something must be wrong with me'* even as adults.

"Any time a situation in our life triggers the memory of this pain or the idea attached to it, we emotionally regress. Thus, we feel and behave like the little kid who first experienced the pain. In fact, that's precisely what happened when you saw my Lorraine cause our father to feel love. You were probably 27 years old, but at that moment you regressed to the two-year-old Jill who felt unloved and acted out all your childhood neediness. And you are still doing it, only this time you are doing it with your husband," I said.

"The idea upon which you based all your relationships represents an interpretation made by a two-year-old kid and has absolutely no basis in fact," I concluded. "Do you see that, Jill?" I asked.

"Yes, I do," she replied. "I made some pretty silly decisions based on those unconscious assumptions, didn't I!"

"Yes, you did, but you made them when you were in pain and when you were too young to know any better. Even though you repressed the pain to get rid of it, the belief kept working in your life at a subconscious level. That's when your soul decided to create some drama in your life so you would bring it to consciousness again and have the opportunity to choose healing once more.

"You attracted people into your life who would confront you directly with your own pain and make you re-live the original experience through them," I continued.

"That's what Jeff is doing right now. Of course, I am not saying he is doing this consciously. He really isn't. He is probably more perplexed at his own behavior than are you. Remember, this is a soul-to-soul transaction. His soul knows about your original pain and is aware that you will not heal it without going through the experience again.

"Wow!" Jill said, and took deep breath. She relaxed her body for the first time since we had begun talking about the situation.

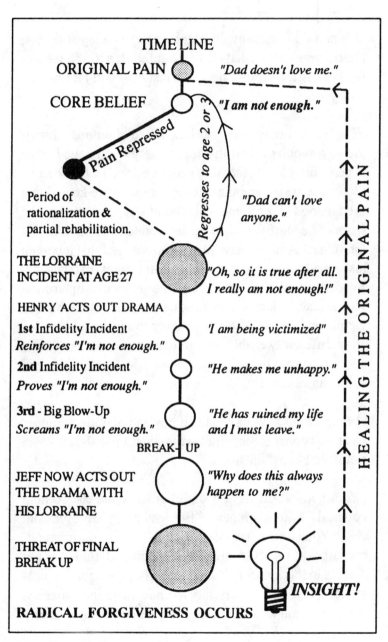

Fig. 1: Jill's Healing Process

"It's certainly a totally different way of looking at things, but do you know what? I feel lighter. It's as if a weight has been lifted off my shoulders just by talking it through with you."

"That's because your energy has shifted" I replied. "Imagine how much of your life-force energy you have had to expend just keeping the story about Dad and Lorraine alive. Plus, imagine the amount of energy required to keep down the feelings of grief and resentment wrapped around the story. The tears you shed earlier enabled you to release a lot of that. And you have just acknowledged that it was all just a made-up story anyway — what a relief that must be. In addition, you've had a lot of energy locked up around Jeff — making him wrong, making yourself wrong, being a victim, and so on. Just being willing to see the whole situation differently enables you to release all that energy and allow it to move through you. No wonder you feel lighter!" I said, and smiled.

"What would have happened if, instead of understanding what was going on underneath the situation with Jeff, I had simply left him?" Jill asked.

"Your soul would have brought in someone else to help you heal," I quickly replied. "But, you didn't leave him, did you? You came here, instead. You have to understand, this trip was no accident. There are no such things as accidents in this system. You — or rather your soul — created this trip, this opportunity to understand the dynamics of the situation with Jeff. Your soul guided you here. John's soul created a trip at this particular time to make it possible for you to come with him."

"And what about the two Lorraines," Jill wondered. "How did that happen? Surely, that's just a coincidence."

"There are no coincidences in this system either. Just know that your souls, and the souls of others, conspired to create this situation, and notice how perfect it was that a person named Lorraine was involved in the original occasion and in this one. It couldn't have been a more perfect clue. It's hard to imagine that it wasn't set up somehow, don't you agree?" I said.

"So, what do I do with this now," asked Jill. "It's true that I feel lighter, but what do I do when I go home and see Jeff?"

"There really is very little for you to do," I answered. "From this point on, it's more a question or how you feel inside yourself. Do you understand that you are no longer a victim? Do you understand that Jeff is no longer a persecutor? Do you see that the situation was exactly what you needed and wanted? Do you feel how much that man loves you — at the soul level, I mean?

"What do you mean?" Jill asked.

"He was willing to do whatever it took to get you to the point where you could look again at your belief about yourself and see that it was untrue. Do you realize how much

31

discomfort he was willing to endure to help you? He is not naturally a cruel man, so it must have been hard for him. Few men could have done that for you while risking losing you in the process. Jeff, or Jeff's soul, truly is an angel for you. When you really understand this, you will feel so grateful to him! Plus, you will stop sending out messages that you are unlovable. You will have the ability to let in love perhaps for the first time in your life. You will have forgiven Jeff, because you will be clear that nothing wrong ever took place. It was perfect in every sense.

"And, I promise you this," I continued. "Jeff is already changing as we speak and dropping his bizarre behavior. His soul is already be picking up that you have forgiven him and healed your misperception about yourself. As you change your energy, his changes too. You're connected energetically. Distance is irrelevant."

Getting back to her question, I said, "So, you won't have to do anything special when you get home. In fact, I want you to promise me that you won't do anything at all when you get back. In particular, do not, under any circumstances, share with him this new way of looking at the situation. I want you to see how everything will be different automatically simply as a consequence of you changing your perception.

"You will feel changed as well," I added. "You will find yourself feeling more peaceful, more centered and more relaxed. You will have a knowingness that will seem strange to Jeff for a while. It will take time for your relationship with him to adjust, and it may still be difficult for a while, but this issue will resolve now," I concluded with conviction.

Jill and I reviewed this new way of looking at her situation many times before she returned home to England. It is always difficult for someone in the middle of an emotional upset to shift into a Radical Forgiveness perspective. In fact, getting to a place where Radical Forgiveness can truly take place often requires a great deal of integration and repetitive reinforcement. To help my sister, I introduced her to some breathing techniques that help release emotion and integrate new ways of being and asked her to complete a Radical Forgiveness worksheet. (See Section Four, Tools For Radical Forgiveness.)

The day she left, Jill obviously was nervous about going back to the situation she had left behind. As she walked down the tunneled ramp to her airplane, she looked back and tried to wave confidently, but I knew she was scared that she might lose her newfound understanding and get drawn back into the drama.

Apparently the meeting with Jeff went well. Jill requested that he not question her immediately about what had happened while she was away and to give her space for a few days to get settled. However, she immediately noticed a difference in him. He was attentive, kind and considerate — more like the Jeff she had known before this whole episode began.

Over the next couple of days, Jill told Jeff she no longer blamed him for anything, nor did she want him to change in any way. She said she had learned that it was she who needed to take responsibility for her own feelings and that she would deal with whatever came up for her in her own way without making him wrong. She elaborated not at all and did not try to explain herself.

Things went on well for some days after Jill's return home, and Jeff's behavior with his daughter, Lorraine, changed dramatically. In fact, everything seemed to be getting back to normal with regard to that relationship, but the atmosphere between Jeff and Jill remained tense and their communication limited.

About two weeks later, the situation came to a head. Jill looked at Jeff and said quietly, "I feel like I've lost my best friend."

"So do I," he replied.

For the first time in months they connected. They hugged each other and began to cry. "Let's talk," Jill said. "I've got to tell you what I learned with Colin in America. It's going to sound weird to you at first, but I want to share it with you. You don't have to believe it. I just want you to hear me. Are you willing?"

"I'll do whatever it takes," replied Jeff. "I know something important happened to you there, and I want to know what it was. You have changed, and I like what I see. You are not the same person you were when you stepped on the airplane with John. So, tell me what happened."

Jill talked and talked. She explained the dynamics of Radical Forgiveness as best she could in a way Jeff could understand. She felt strong and powerful — sure of herself and her understanding, secure and clear in her mind.

Jeff, a practical man who always is skeptical of anything that cannot be rationally explained, did not resist this time — and was indeed quite receptive to the ideas that Jill asked him to consider. He voiced openness to the idea that there might be a spiritual world beneath everyday reality and, given that, saw a certain logic in the Radical Forgiveness concept. He didn't accept it totally, but he nevertheless was willing to listen, to consider and to see how it had changed Jill.

After the discussion, they both felt their love had been rekindled and that their relationship had a good chance of surviving. They made no promises, though, and agreed to keep talking to each other while they watched how their relationship progressed.

It did, indeed, progress quite well. Jeff still fawned over his daughter, Lorraine, to a degree but not as much as before. Jill found she cared hardly at all even when he did behave in this manner. It certainly did not trigger her to regress emotionally and react from old beliefs about herself. Within a month of their conversation about Radical Forgiveness, all of Jeff's past behavioral pattern with

35

Lorraine stopped. In turn, Lorraine didn't call or visit as often; she got on with her life. Everything slowly returned to normal.

Looking back, had Jill's soul not brought her to Atlanta to create the opportunity for us to have our conversation, I feel sure she and Jeff would have separated. In the grand scheme of things, that would have been all right, too. Jill simply would have found someone else with whom to recreate the drama and another opportunity to heal. As it was, she took the opportunity to heal this time, and stayed in the relationship. At the time of writing, they remain together and apparently very happily married. Like every other couple they continue to create dramas in their lives — but they know now how to see them as healing opportunities and to move through them quickly and with grace.

PART TWO

Conversations On
Radical Forgiveness

2: Underlying Assumptions

Since all theories are based upon certain assumptions, it is important to have an understanding of the spiritual assumptions underlying the theory of Radical Forgiveness.

Before looking at these though, it is worth noting that even the most widely accepted theories are based on assumptions for which there is very little hard evidence. For example, did you know that not one shred of evidence exists to support Darwin's Theory of Evolution? Historically, that theory probably ranks as one of the biggest assumptions ever made. It serves as the basic assumption behind all biological science and as the very foundation on which much of our accepted scientific *truth* rests. However, the fact that no evidence exists to prove this assumption true does not mean that the theory is invalid or not useful.

We can say the same of the basic assumptions handed down throughout the ages about God, human nature, and the spiritual universe. These form the foundation for Radical Forgiveness and Radical Forgiveness Therapy (RFT). While there is little hard scientific evidence to support their validity, such assumptions have been handed down to us as *universal truths, or principles,* for centuries and have formed the foundation for many great spiritual traditions throughout the world.

Although the following outlines of these assumptions will be sufficient to enable you to follow the logic in the pages that follow, each assumption is expanded upon in length at various other places in the book.

Assumptions:

- Contrary to most Western religious thought, we are *not* human beings having an occasional spiritual experience; rather *we are spiritual beings having a human experience.* (An important and *radical* distinction!)

- We have bodies that die, but we have immortal souls that transcend death.

- While our bodies and our senses tell us we are separate individuals, we are all **one**. We all individually vibrate as part of a single whole.

- Vibrationally, we live in two worlds simultaneously:
    1) The World of Divine Truth.
    2) The World of Humanity.
  *Note: The first is **real**, the second is **illusion**.*

- We have chosen to fully experience the energy of the World of Humanity in order to heal the wounds of our soul.

- When our spirits were all one with God, we

experimented with a thought that separation was possible. We became trapped in that experiment, which became the illusion (sometimes called a dream), that we now live. It is an illusion because the separation did not happen. We only think it did. The belief that we are separate from God caused the birth of the Ego.

• The Ego protects us from the overwhelming guilt that we felt when we separated — as well as the fear of God's wrath — through the mechanisms of repression and projection. (see Chapter 6.)

• When we decided to experiment with physical incarnation (our way of separating), God gave us total **free will** to live this experiment in any way we chose and to find for ourselves the way back home.

• We come in to the physical life experience with a mission — to fully experience a particular energy pattern so we can feel the feelings associated with that pattern and then transform that energy through love. (see Chapter 10).

• We keep on coming back lifetime after lifetime, usually with the same soul group, to balance karmic energy and to heal our wounded souls.

• Life is not a random event. It is entirely purposeful and provides for the unfoldment of a divine plan with opportunities to make choices and decisions in every moment.

- We create our reality through the Law of Cause and Effect. Thoughts are causes that show up in our world as physical effects. Reality is an outplaying of our consciousness. Our world offers a mirror of our beliefs. (see Chapter 8.)

- We get precisely what we want in our life. How we judge what we get determines whether we experience life as either painful or joyful.

- Through relationship we grow and learn. Through relationship we heal and are returned to wholeness. We need others to mirror our misperceptions and our projections and to help us bring repressed material to consciousness for healing.

- Through the Law of Resonance, we attract people who resonate with our issues so we might heal on them. For example, if abandonment is our issue, we will tend to attract people who abandon us. In that sense they serve as our teachers. (see Chapter 7).

- Physical reality is an illusion created by our five senses. Matter consists of interrelating energy fields vibrating at different frequencies. (see Chapter 12).

- We have subtle bodies as well as physical bodies. Our physical body vibrates at the frequency of matter (the World of Humanity), while the highest two of the five subtle bodies vibrate closer to the frequency of the World of Divine Truth.

3: Worlds Apart

There is a big difference between Radical Forgiveness and all other forms of forgiveness. While Radical Forgiveness takes the position that there is nothing to forgive, all other forms of forgiveness — for which I have coined the term *Mock Forgiveness* — take it as a given that something wrong happened. In other words:

*With **RADICAL FORGIVENESS** willingness to forgive is present and the victim consciousness is **dropped.***

*With **MOCK FORGIVENESS** willingness to forgive is present but the victim consciousness is **maintained.***

(**Victim Consciousness** — the conviction that someone else has done something bad to you, and, as a direct result, they are responsible for the lack of peace and happiness in your life).

There is a third distinction that, while not forgiveness at all, needs mentioning since a lot of what passes for forgiveness falls into this category. This is Pseudo Forgiveness.

***PSEUDO FORGIVENESS** shows a lack of willingness to forgive and **increases** victim consciousness.*

Why *Mock* Forgiveness?

Logically, I could have referred to that we ordinarily refer to as forgiveness as *ordinary forgiveness*. However, I just couldn't bring myself to call any genuine attempt at forgiveness *ordinary*. Forgiveness is heroic and in that sense always *extraordinary*. In my search for a term that would make the right distinction, I found it in the culinary arts.

Turtle Soup vs. Mock Turtle Soup

If you have ever tasted mock-turtle soup you will know that it is a wonderful soup. However, when we order mock-turtle soup we do so with the full knowledge that it will not contain any turtle — just ingredients that mimic the taste of turtle. Even though it is not *real* in that sense, we can appreciate mock-turtle soup for the great soup it is in its own right. (There is a good recipe for mock-turtle soup given in Appendix 2. Try it and you will see what I mean!)

Different Worlds — Different Perspectives

As with the ersatz soup, Mock Forgiveness, while not the *real thing*, is extremely beneficial when used in the context of a certain set of beliefs — beliefs that are firmly rooted in the physical world and everyday human reality. Radical Forgiveness, on the other hand, is the *real* thing because it is rooted in the metaphysical reality of the world of Spirit — what I call the World of Divine Truth.

This makes the distinction between Radical and Mock

Forgiveness easier to draw, because we know that in each case we look through completely different lenses. We approach each one from a totally different point of view.

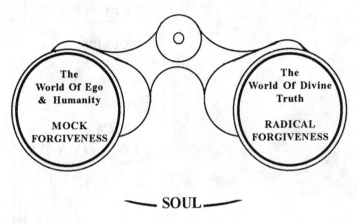

Figure 2: Perspectives On Two Worlds.

Because we live with one foot in each world (since we are spiritual beings having a human experience), we can reference situations through either, or both, lenses. While being fully grounded in the World of Humanity, we are connected to the World of Divine Truth through our soul. Since the importance of this distinction cannot be over-emphasized, some further explanation might be helpful here.

These worlds represent two ends of a vibrational scale. When we vibrate at a low frequency, our bodies become dense and we exist only in the World of Humanity. When we vibrate at a high level, which makes our bodies become lighter, we exist also in the World of Divine Truth. Depending upon our vibration at any moment, we move up and down the scale toward one world or the other.

45

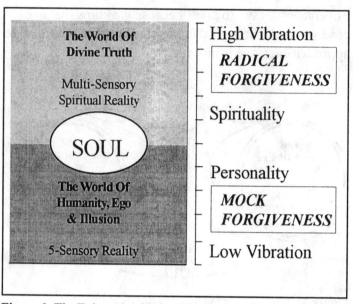

Figure 3. The Existential Chain of Being

The World of Humanity represents the world of objective reality we see as *outside ourselves*. As a world of form, it provides the setting in which we live our everyday human lives, as well as the reality we experience through our five senses. It holds the energy patterns of death, change, fear, limitation, and duality. This world provides us with the environment in which we, as spiritual beings, can experience being human. This means having a physical body and working with (and possibly transcending) these particular energies.

The World of Divine Truth, on the other hand, has no physical form and already carries the energy pattern of eternal life, immutability, infinite abundance, love, and oneness with God. Even though we cannot perceive this world with our five senses, and scarcely possess the mental capacity to comprehend it, we can get enough of a sense of it to know that it is real. Such activities as prayer, meditation and Radical Forgiveness, all of which increase our vibrational level, allow us to access the World of Divine Truth.

These *existential realms* differ not in terms of place or time but solely in their vibrational level. The study of quantum physics has proven that all reality consists of energy patterns and that consciousness sustains these energy patterns. Thus, the world of form exists as dense concentrations of energy vibrating at frequencies we can experience through our physical senses. On the other hand, we experience the World of Divine Truth as an inner knowing and sensations.

Because these two worlds exist on the same continuum, we do not live sometimes in one and sometimes in the other. We live in both worlds at the same time. However, which world we experience at any given moment depends upon our awareness of them. Obviously, as human beings our consciousness resonates easily with the World of Humanity. Our senses naturally pull us into that world and convince us that it is real. Though some people are less grounded in the world of objective reality than others, human beings, on the whole, are firmly entrenched at this end of the continuum.

We possess a limited awareness of the World of Divine Truth, but this appears to be by design. Our soul enters

47

into this world to experience being human — thus our memory and awareness of the World of Divine Truth must be limited to allow us the full experience. We would not be able to take on fully the energies of change, fear, death, limitation, and duality that characterize this world if we knew they were illusory. If we retained this knowledge, we would deny ourselves the opportunity to transcend these states and *to discover* that they are, indeed, simply illusions. By forgetting who we are when we take on a physical body, we give ourselves the chance to remember that we are spiritual beings having a physical experience.

During a gathering in Atlanta in 1990, I heard Gerald Jampowlsky, a well known author and authority on "A Course In Miracles," tell a story about a couple returning home from the hospital after giving birth to their second child. This wonderful true story illustrates the fact that we do have a true knowing of our connection with God and our own soul but that we forget it fairly quickly after taking on a body. This couple was conscious of the need to include their three-year-old daughter in the celebration of the new baby's homecoming. However, they felt perturbed by her insistence that she be allowed go alone into the room with the baby. To honor her request, yet oversee the situation, they switched on the baby monitor so they could at least hear what was going on, if not see it. What they heard astounded them. The little girl went straight to the crib, looked through the bars at the newborn child, and said, "Baby, tell me about God. I'm beginning to forget."

In spite of the veil we lower over the memory of our one-ness with God, which the above story suggests might become fully drawn around the age of three, as humans we are not denied a connection to the World of Divine Truth. Our soul carries a vibration that resonates with the World of Divine Truth and connects us to that world. Soul normally experiences no limitation. However, when it incarnates, the soul creates a personality that carries the particular characteristics it needs to experience healing. Taking on this personality, in part, causes us to forget our connection to the World of Divine Truth. We can be in touch with our soul through practices like meditation, prayer, yoga, breathwork, dancing, and chanting. Through such practices we raise our vibration enough to resonate with that of the World of Divine Truth.

Mock Forgiveness differs from Radical Forgiveness in that it holds on to victim consciousness — which can exist only in the World of Humanity. However, Mock Forgiveness, like mock-turtle soup, still has great value in its own right. It calls upon the finest of human qualities and characteristics, such as compassion, mercy, tolerance, humility and kindness. Joan Borysenko calls forgiveness "the exercise of compassion."* What can be more healing than true compassion? That's good soup by any standards! However, while Radical Forgiveness goes to the very core and brings about transformation, Mock Forgiveness is palliative in nature and built on the shifting sands of illusion.

Though the difference between the definition of Radical

---

* "Guilt is the Teacher, Love is the Lesson," Warner Books, 1990

Forgiveness and Mock Forgiveness comes down to one word, a huge gap exists between them in terms of the level of consciousness experienced by the individual forgiving. In this respect, the two types of forgiveness remain literally worlds apart. They each demand a different way of looking at the world and at life. Clearly, Mock Forgiveness offers itself as *a way of living in the world* while Radical Forgiveness is nothing less than *a spiritual path.*

Why *Radical?*

I adopted the term *Radical* to distinguish clearly this form of forgiveness from others. The term describes something, if not exactly extreme, certainly way beyond what most people consider the norm. We are used to seeing forgiveness treated with undue sentimentality and smalz, not to mention hypocrisy. In addition to giving it a very 'radical' definition, I am presenting Radical Forgiveness as being quite hard-nosed, disciplined and practical, as well as totally essential to all aspects of our lives. It is necessary for our happiness, our health, our evolution, and, indeed, our very survival. It liberates us from the scourge of co-dependency and the tyranny of the not-so-loveable brat we are pleased to call our wounded inner-child. It frees us from our past and has the potential to propel us into the next phase of our spiritual evolution. It teaches us very powerfully that, if we want to grow, forgiveness is in no way optional.

According to The New Universal Dictionary, the term radical also means *pertaining to the orginal or the root; fundamental.* Radical Forgiveness goes to the very core of what originally gave rise to the victim consciousness and seeks to transform it. It is truly fundamental in that sense.

In terms of our capacity to heal ourselves and to evolve spiritually, Radical Forgiveness offers extraordinary potential to transform consciousness, and this potential far exceeds what is possible with Mock Forgiveness.

Yet, we must recognize that we all still live in the World of Humanity, and at certain times we will fall short of Radical Forgiveness' spiritual ideal. When we find ourselves immersed in our own pain, for example, it becomes virtually impossible for us to move into Radical Forgiveness. When we have recently experienced harm at the hand of another, such as when we have just been raped, we cannot be expected to accept, in that moment, that the experience was something we wanted and that it represents the unfoldment of a divine plan. We will not have the essential listening necessary to hold that vision. It can only come later in moments of quiet reflection, not in the heat of anger and in the immediate aftermath of a trauma.

You Cannot Heal What You Do Not Feel

Before we can begin to forgive, we must feel the pain fully and accept the feelings just the way they are. Then we can try to find the willingness to forgive. In the beginning such willingness may only be mustered in the context of Mock Forgiveness — and getting even that far might take a long time. In this sense perhaps, Mock Forgiveness may represent an interim stage in the process.

51

Pseudo Forgiveness

Lacking authenticity, Pseudo Forgiveness is just neatly packaged judgment and concealed resentment masquerading as forgiveness. However, the line between this and Mock Forgiveness may not be easy to determine and will depend on the consciousness of the person forgiving.

Examples

The following examples are listed in order of descending clarity, beginning with ones that are obviously false and ending with those that come close to Mock Forgiveness.

- *Forgiving out of a sense of obligation*— This is totally inauthentic, yet many of us forgive from this place. We think of forgiveness as the *right* thing or even the *spiritual* thing to do. We think we *ought* to forgive.

- *Forgiving out of a sense of righteousness*— This is the antithesis of forgiveness. If you forgive people because you think you are right and they are stupid, or because you pity them, that is pure arrogance.

- *Bestowing forgiveness or pardoning*— This is pure self-delusion. We do not possess the power to bestow forgiveness on anyone. When we bestow forgiveness, we *play God.* Forgiveness is not something we control — it just happens in the heart when we are willing.

- *Pretending Forgiveness*— pretending that we are not

angry about something when we actually are angry provides not so much an opportunity to forgive but to deny our anger. This represents a form of self- invalidation. When we do this we allow others to treat us like the proverbial doormat. Such behavior usually stems from a fear of not forgiving, of being abandoned, or from a belief that expressing anger is unacceptable.

• *Forgive and Forget*— This simply creates denial. Forgiveness is never simple erasure. Wise people forgive but *do not* forget. They strive to appreciate the gift inherent in the situation and to remember the lesson it taught them.

• *Making Excuses*—When we forgive, we often do it with explanations or by making excuses for the person we are forgiving. For example, we might say about our parents, "My father abused me, because he was abused by his own parents. He was doing the best he could."

Forgiveness should be about letting go of the past and refusing to be controlled by it. If an explanation helps one to let go it might be helpful to that extent, though an explanation does not remove the idea that something wrong happened. Therefore, at best, it can only be Mock Forgiveness. It also possesses a certain righteousness, which may mask anger. On the other hand, understanding why someone did what they did and having empathy for them connects us again to our own imperfection and opens the door to feeling compassion and mercy — also Mock Forgiveness.

- *Forgiving the person but not condoning the behavior.* This largely intellectual approach may only masquerade as forgiveness, because it remains judgmental and self-righteous. It also has practical and semantic problems. How do you separate a murderer from the act of murder?

This last one also raises the question of *accountability and responsibility.* Neither Radical Forgiveness nor Mock Forgiveness relieves anyone from responsibility in this world. We are spiritual beings having a human experience, and, as such, we must experience accountability for our actions.

When we create circumstances that hurt other people, we must accept that in the World of Humanity there are consequences for such actions. *From a Radical Forgiveness standpoint, we would say that all parties involved in the situation are getting what they need. Nevertheless, they are still consequences.*

I am often asked whether, in a situation where someone has done us harm and where the normal reaction would be to seek redress through the courts, a forgiving person would actually take that course of action? The answer is, "*Yes.*" We live in the World of Humanity, which operates within the parameters of the Law of Cause and Effect, which states that for every action there is a correspondingly equal reaction. Thus, early on we learn that our actions have consequences. If we were never held to be accountable for the harm we do, forgiveness would be meaningless and valueless. With no accountability put upon us, it would appear as if, no matter what we did, no one cared. Such action or attitude offers no compassion whatsoever. For instance, children always interpret *rightful* parental discipline applied appropriately as caring and loving. Conversely, they interpret being given total license by their parents as non-caring.

However, the extent to which we respond to other people's actions with a sense of righteous indignation, grievance, revenge, and resentment, rather than with a genuine desire to balance the scales with regard to principles of fairness, freedom and respect for others, determines our level of forgiveness. Righteousness and revenge lower our vibration. Conversely, defense of principles raises our vibration. The higher the vibration, the closer we come to Divine Truth and the more able we are to forgive radically.

I recently heard best-selling author, Alan Cohen, tell a story that illustrates this point well. A friend of his once got involved in circumstances that resulted in a girl's death. For her wrongful death, he was imprisoned for many years. He accepted the responsibility for what had happened and behaved in every way as a model prisoner. However, the girl's father, a rich and influential man with friends in high places, made a vow to keep this man locked up for as many years as possible. So, every time this man became eligible for parole, the girl's father spent a great deal of time and money pulling every political string possible to make sure parole was denied. After numerous such occurences, Cohen asked his friend how he felt about being denied parole because of this man's efforts to keep

DISTINCTIONS

MOCK FORGIVENESS		RADICAL FORGIVENESS
World of Humanity (EGO)	Vs.	World of Divine Truth
Low vibratory rate	Vs.	High vibratory rate
Something wrong happened	Vs.	Nothing wrong (or right) happened
Judgment based	Vs.	Value free and blame-free
Past orientaton	Vs.	Present time orientation
Need to figure it all out	Vs.	Willingness to accept & surrender
Victim consciousness prevails	Vs.	Seeing the gift in the situation
Acknowledges human imperfection	Vs.	Sees perfection in the imperfection
What happened happened *(true)*	Vs.	Symbolic meaning of it *(truth)*
References physical reality only	Vs.	References metaphysical realities
Problem still is 'out there'	Vs.	Problem is with me - my error
Letting go of resentment	Vs.	Embracing the resentment
Compassion for the other person	Vs.	Compassion for myself
Tolerance of imperfection	Vs.	Gratitude for the gift.
Cannot be willed	Vs.	Willingness - to see it differently
'Shit happens'	Vs.	There are no accidents
Life is a series of random events	Vs.	Life is purposeful and intelligent
Personality and Ego in control	Vs.	Soul orchestrating a divine plan
This life only	Vs.	Reincarnation, mission & karma*
Lower four chakras	Vs.	Higher four chakras*

• For further explanation, see Chapter 14, 'Articles of Faith.'

Figure 4: Distinctions Between Radical & Mock Forgiveness

him in prison. The man said he forgave the girl's father every day of his life and prayed for him, because he realized that it was the father who was in prison, not himself.

In truth, the father who was unable to get beyond his rage, sadness and grief, was controlled by his need for revenge. He could not escape the prison of his own victimhood. Even Mock Forgiveness was beyond him. Cohen's friend on the other hand, refused to be a victim and saw love as the only possibility. His vibration was higher and he was able to practice Radical Forgiveness.

Getting back to the issue of whether or not to seek redress through the courts, we should seek to make others accountable for their actions. Remember, though, that once we decide to sue, we must "pray for the S.O.B." and for ourselves. (By the way, we do not have to like someone to forgive them!) In other words, we turn the matter over to our Higher Power. We recognize that Divine Love operates in every situation and that each person receives exactly what they want. We recognize that perfection resides somewhere in the situation, even if it is not apparent at the time.

It is worth remembering, too, that if we possess a Radical Forgiveness consciousness, things seldom end up in a court of law. Our energy transforms the situation long before things reach that level of confrontation.

Characteristics of Radical Forgiveness

• *Radical Forgiveness* aligns with the vibration of the World of Divine Truth *not* with the World of Humanity. However, with Divine assistance, it can be accessed from the World of Humanity through our soul.

• *Radical Forgiveness* sees the World of Humanity as an illusion -- a direct reflection of our judgments and beliefs about "how things are" in the objective world. To forgive, we simply must shift our perception in the direction of *truth*.

• *Radical Forgiveness* requires the willingness to have our minds changed about a situation and the humility and wisdom to ask for Divine help in doing so.

• *Radical Forgiveness* requires the willingness to see the perfection in every situation (knowing no right or wrong is involved) regardless of how it seems and to feel the love that always flows beneath the apparent circumstances of the situation.

• *Radical Forgiveness* recognizes that problems do not exist *out there* but exist only within ourselves as misperceptions. All problems are lovingly self-created as opportunities to learn and to heal.

• *Radical Forgiveness* recognizes that what we attack in others represents what we have condemned in ourselves, repressed, denied, and projected onto others.

- *Radical Forgiveness* involves undoing (taking back) the projection. This can be considered self-forgiveness, because the way we see others represents how we see ourselves.

- *Radical Forgiveness* recognizes that we cannot will or bestow forgiveness. Any kind of forgiveness can happen only with the help of a Higher Power. Our work always involves surrendering to the perfection of the situation.

- *Radical Forgiveness* sees death as illusionary and our human evolutionary journey as involving reincarnation, karma and a specific mission for our life.

- *Radical Forgiveness* does not demand that we change anything in the world. Rather it asks for a transformation of the energy around the circumstances of the world. Paradoxically, this means accepting and loving these circumstances just the way they are so we can drop our need to sustain them.

- *Radical Forgiveness* represents a direct threat to the Ego. The Ego uses projection, repression and the victim archetype as the dynamic for its own survival. Forgiveness that has the blessing of the Ego can never be true forgiveness.

Mock Forgiveness By Contrast

- **Mock Forgiveness** is firmly rooted in the World of Humanity. In the same way that the World of Humanity holds the energy of duality, so Mock Forgiveness polarizes and judges everything as either good or bad, right or wrong. *Radical Forgiveness takes the view that there is no right/wrong or good/bad. Only our thinking makes it so.*

- **Mock Forgiveness** always begins with the assumption that something wrong took place, and someone 'did something' to someone else. The victim archetype remains operative. *Radical Forgiveness begins with the belief that nothing wrong happened, and there are no victims in any situation.*

- **Mock Forgiveness** is effective to the extent that it calls upon the highest human virtues, such as compassion, tolerance, kindness, mercy, and humility. These qualities point towards forgiveness and have healing potential. However, in and of themselves, they are not forgiveness.

- **Mock Forgiveness** depends upon our own capacity to feel compassion, so it is limited in this regard. No matter how much compassion or tolerance we muster for someone like Hitler, and no matter how much we empathize with the pain of his upbringing, nothing enables us to forgive him (using Mock Forgiveness) for the mass genocide of six million Jews. *Radical Forgiveness has no limits whatsoever and is completely unconditional. If*

*Radical Forgiveness cannot forgive Hitler, it can for-
give nobody. Like unconditional love, it's all or nothing.*

• With **Mock Forgiveness**, the Ego and our personality-
self calls the shots. Hence, the problem always appears
'out-there' with someone else. Mock Forgiveness works
in cahoots with the Ego to maintain this projection. *With
Radical Forgiveness, the finger points the other way
— the problem lies 'in here,' with me.*

• **Mock Forgiveness** believes in the reality of the physical world, in the complete integrity of 'what happens'
and always tries to 'figure it all out' and, thus, control
the situation. *Radical Forgiveness recognizes the illusion, sees that what happened was just a story and
responds by surrendering to the perfection of the situation.*

• **Mock Forgiveness** does not factor in ideas of reincarnation or the notion of a spiritual mission and maintains
its belief in, and fear of, death. *Radical Forgiveness
sees death as an illusion and takes the view that life
is eternal and that we incarnate many times for specific purposes.*

• **Mock Forgiveness** views life as a problem to be solved
or punishment to be avoided. It experiences life as a
random set of circumstances that just happen to us for
no reason — thus, the origin of the popular bumper
sticker, 'Shit happens!' *Radical Forgiveness sees life
as entirely purposeful and motivated by love.*

61

- **Mock Forgiveness** recognizes the inherent imperfection of human beings but fails to see the *perfection in the imperfection.* It cannot live in that kind of paradox. *Radical Forgiveness exemplifies that paradox.*

- Whereas Radical Forgiveness *always* carries a high vibration, since it references the world of Divine Truth, **Mock Forgiveness** *may* carry a similarly high vibration. It does so when calling upon some of the highest of human virtues, like kindness, humility, compassion, patience, and tolerance. Using prayer also raises its vibration, as does activation of the 4th chakra, the heart. Anything less than this can be only pseudo forgiveness, which carries a low vibration. *The heart serves as the portal through which we begin the journey of raising our vibration to connect with the world of Divine Truth and experience Radical Forgiveness.*

- High Vibrational **Mock Forgiveness** recognizes the profundity of the spiritual insight that we *all* are imperfect and that imperfection characterizes the nature of humanity. When we look at a wrongdoer through these eyes, we can say in all humility and with tolerance and compassion, "There, but for the Grace of God, go I." We own that we, too, are completely capable of whatever the accused person has done. If we are acquainted with our shadow-self, we know that we all have within us the potential to cause harm, to murder, to rape, to abuse children, and to annihilate six million people. This knowledge allows us to call forth our humility and makes us kind and merciful not only to the accused but to ourselves, for in them we recognize our own inherent imperfection, our own shadow. This recognition brings us very close to actually taking back that which we projected — the vital first step in Radical Forgiveness. *Radical Forgiveness also lovingly sees the imperfection inherent in human beings but sees the perfection in the imperfection.*

• **Mock Forgiveness** recognizes that forgiveness cannot be willed or bestowed. We must *be willing* to forgive and to give the situation over to our Higher Power. Forgiveness comes not from effort but from being open to experiencing it. *Radical Forgiveness is no different in this respect.*

4: Radical Forgiveness Therapy

The only thing unusual about the story told in Chapter 1 is that it happens to feature my own relatives. In truth, there are many other stories I could have chosen to illustrate Radical Forgiveness, but insofar as it is typical of many so-called relationship problems, this story provides a good example of how Radical Forgiveness can be applied to the quite ordinary problems of every day life. It also demonstrates its viability as a radical alternative to traditional counseling and psychotherapy.

Furthermore, this story amply demonstrates the one simple principle underlying Radical Forgiveness that differentiates it from Mock Forgiveness:

Without exception, everything that happens to us is divinely guided, purposeful and for our greater good.

To the extent that we are able to acknowledge this and to realize that what we receive in our lives represents perfect feedback, we can stop being victims and feel the support of the Universe.

You will recall from the last chapter that where other forms of forgiveness always assume that someone did something wrong, or bad, that has to be forgiven, Radical Forgiveness recognizes that nothing wrong, or bad, ever took place; paradoxically therefore, there is nothing to forgive.

Surely you will agree that this qualifies as a radical idea and that this type of forgiveness is indeed radical. After all, Jill's original perception of the situation with Jeff, and of all prior situations with her previous husband, certainly did not take this form. Indeed she felt that what had occurred was *self-evidently* wrong or bad. Most people would have agreed with her. However, as we saw, the healing occurred for her only when she realized that, in fact, there was no right or wrong in any of the situations and that she was clearly not being victimized by anyone. On the contrary, at every moment Divine guidance was helping her heal an earlier misperception and related false belief system that for years had prevented her from expressing her true self. Each situation was, on that basis, a gift of grace.

Additionally, the story demonstrates how difficult making that shift in perception can be. Even with fairly obvious clues, it took a lot of discussion and a lot of processing of emotional pain before Jill became open to understanding a different interpretation. This especially was true of her former husband's supposed infidelity.

Imagine how tough it might be to sell the idea of Radical Forgiveness to a holocaust victim or to someone who has just been raped or otherwise violently abused. Indeed, much of RFT's preliminary work involves creating a willingness to even look at the *possibility* of there being perfection in what happened. Even then, depending on the circumstances, developing such a receptivity can take a long time and almost always requires a great deal of emotional release work first.

Some people may never get to the point where they become receptive — at least not in their current lifetime. They simply may never get beyond their feelings of victimhood. On the other hand, those who do find themselves able to see, even for a moment, the perfection in their situation, are empowered to release their feelings of victimhood and to become free.

Therein lies the power of this work, for, as we shall see in later chapters, releasing victimhood provides the key to health, personal power and spiritual evolution. We have been addicted to the victim archetype for eons, and as we move into the Aquarian Age (the next 2,000-year period of spiritual evolution), we must answer the call to let go of the past, release the victim archetype and be more aware of life occurring in the moment.

There are some prerequisites, however, to doing so. First, the receptivity that Radical Forgiveness ultimately depends upon requires our being open to seeing things from a spiritual standpoint. It references no particular religion and excludes none, but it does require at least a belief in a Higher Power or Higher Intelligence and the idea of a

The Evolution Of Consciousness Into The Aquarian Age

OLD CONSCIOUSNESS		EVOLVING CONSCIOUSNESS
Piscean	vs.	Aquarian
Male Energy - Zeuss & Apollo	vs.	Female energy (Divine Androgeny)
5-sensory human beings	vs.	Multi-sensory human beings
Humans having a spiritual experience	vs.	Spiritual beings having a human experience
Reality based on Newtonian Physics	vs.	Reality based on Quantum physics
Physical universe	vs.	Holographic universe
Physical reality	vs.	Metaphysical realities
Human observers of a world 'out there'.	vs.	Humans as co-creators of reality
Evolution as 'Survival of The Fittest.'	vs.	Evolution as 'Spiritual Advancement.'
Biology & Chemistry	vs.	Bio-energetic fields
Externalized power and control.	vs.	Authentic personal power from within.
Religious dogmas	vs.	Personal spirituality
Stable, fixed institutions.	vs.	Constantly changing organic structures.
Rational scientific thought	vs.	Intuitive, open-ended thought
Control centered interaction	vs.	Heart centered interaction
Lower four chakras dominant	vs.	Upper four chakras dominant
Allopathic, high-tech medicine	vs.	Holistic, energy-based medicine
Man dominating/controlling Nature	vs.	Nature respected and honored
Personal survival and success in world	vs.	Spiritual purpose and life mission
Singular life	vs.	Reincarnation and karma
Predominance of Personality or EGO	vs.	Predominance of SOUL
• Fear based consciousness	vs.	• Love based consciousness
• Belief in Separateness	vs.	• Belief in Oneness
• Sorrow, shame, indifference	vs.	• Wisdom and caring
• Woundology	vs.	• Intimacy and Healing
• Judges and exploits	vs.	• Accepts as is
• Manipulating/controlling	vs.	• Flows with what is.
Belief that death is real. (mortality)	vs.	Belief that death is illusion. (Immortality)
Belief in scarcity	vs.	Belief in abundance
Belief in danger	vs.	Belief in safety
Coincidence	vs.	Synchronicity
Investment in the physical illusion	vs.	Trust in the symbolic meaning of events
Victim consciousness	vs.	**Forgiveness consciousness**
Socially controlled choices	vs.	Personal responsbility and conscious choice

Mock Forgiveness vs Radical Forgiveness

Fig. 5: Evolution Into The Aquarian Age.

spiritual reality beyond our own physical world. Second, for some aspects of Radical Forgiveness, one would also need to be comfortable with the idea of reincarnation.

Having said that, Radical Forgiveness can be explained in non-threatening terms and in such language as to honor all people's religious beliefs. It can be explained in ways that provide a fit with their existing belief system, thus allowing them to listen. Besides that, a substantial part of Radical Forgiveness Therapy (RFT), does not depend upon mystical or esoteric ideas for its validity. Repression, denial and projection all are concepts firmly rooted in psychological theory dating back to the work of Sigmund Freud, *the father of psychotherapy.* Therefore, these mechanisms can be explained fully in scientific terms.

However, for a person to release the victim archetype, they must comfortably accept certain spiritual assumptions. So much depends upon recognizing the difference between our physical world (The World of Humanity) and the World of Divine Truth, and upon developing a perspective that includes them both. For this reason, a strictly atheistic viewpoint would not allow Radical Forgiveness to occur, nor RFT to work. We shall see that to make Radical Forgiveness a reality in our lives, we need to be comfortable with the idea that we can walk in both worlds simultaneously.

From a therapeutic point of view, insofar as Jill's story actually demonstrates RFT in operation — albeit not in a professional context — amply illustrates how the basic questions being asked by RFT separate it from most other forms of traditional psychotherapy or counseling.

Questions Underlying Traditional Therapy:

1. What is wrong with this person or his/her circumstances?
2. What caused him/her to become this way?
3. How can his/her problem be fixed?

Radical Forgiveness Asks Instead:

1. What is perfect about what is occurring for this person?
2. How is this perfection being revealed?
3. How can the person shift their viewpoint so they can see the perfection in the situation?

These fundamentally different questions require very different mind-sets. Any therapist who adds RFT to his or her tool kit needs to be aware of the distinctions between RFT and traditional therapy and must be able to clearly differentiate them to a client.

By way of illustration, recall that in the beginning of the story with Jill, I acted out of an implicit *agreement* with her that she really did have a problem, that Jeff was the basic cause of it and that the only way to react to it was by trying to find a solution. For quite some time I went down this road with her. Only when I thought the time was right did I suggest the other approach. Then, I had to make it very clear to her that I was shifting the conversation to an entirely different direction and using an alternate set of assumptions.

Mixing the two forms of therapy will not work. The questions and the assumptions underlying the questions are just too different. Indeed, a large proportion of the actual work done in RFT lies in helping the client look at the underlying assumptions and principles so their perception of the situation might shift and become meaningful in a wholly different way.

This actually makes RFT less of a therapy and more of a process of education. The therapist or counselor acts not so much out of a desire to fix someone as to enlighten him or her. Of course, when a person has profound issues and deeply repressed pain with complex defense mechanisms in place, that person needs to work with a qualified psychotherapist who also uses RFT.

Training and certification in RFT is available through the **Radical Forgiveness Therapy Center, Atlanta, Georgia.** This is both for licensed professionals who wish to become certified Radical Forgiveness Practitioners, and for non-professionals who might simply wish to coach others in how to apply Radical Forgiveness to ordinary life-problems. Even in business, Radical Forgiveness is a valid concept and an extremely useful tool. **For further details and the toll-free number, see Appendix I.**

5: The Mechanisms of The Ego

To fully understand Radical Forgiveness, we must first understand the mechanism of the Ego and how it created the victim archetype.

The Ego exists only as a deeply-held set of beliefs about who we are in relationship to Spirit. All belief systems quickly become resistant to change, but the Ego is no ordinary belief system. It holds incredible power in our unconscious mind and carries an big block of votes when it comes to making decisions about who we think we are. This belief system is so powerful that it appears to be an entity in its own right — and we have named it the Ego.

The Ego was born when we experimented with the thought of separation from the Divine Source. Our experiment trapped us in that thought, which then became the illusion in which we now live. The illusion, most importantly, includes the belief that we are, indeed, separate and that is what constitutes *the original sin.* In actuality, no separation occurred. Consequently there is no such thing as original sin.

Jesus himself gave us this revelation — the truth about our illusion — in "A Course In Miracles," (Foundation For

Inner Peace, 1973), a three-volume work by Jesus channeled through a lady called Helen Schucman, the purpose of which was to show us the error of the Ego's way and to teach us that the way home to God is through forgiveness. *Interestingly, Helen was a very reluctant channel and never did believe a word of what she channeled.*

At the moment of separation, the Ego made up a story that God had become very angry about our experiment. This immediately created enormous guilt within us. The Ego then elaborated on its story by telling us that God would get even and punish us severely for our great sin. So great was the guilt and the terror created in us by the belief that this story was true, we had no choice but to repress these emotions deep in our unconscious mind. This spared us from the conscious awareness of them.

This tactic worked quite well, yet we retained a great fear that the feelings might rise once again. To remedy this problem, the Ego developed a new belief: that the guilt lay with someone else rather than within ourselves. In other words, we began projecting our guilt on to other people so we could be rid of it entirely. They became our *scapegoats*. Then, to ensure that the guilt stayed with them, we became angry with them and kept up a continuous attack on them.

Herein lies the origin of the victim archetype and the human race's continual need to attack and to defend against each other. After attacking the people onto whom we projected our guilt, we fear them attacking us in return. So,

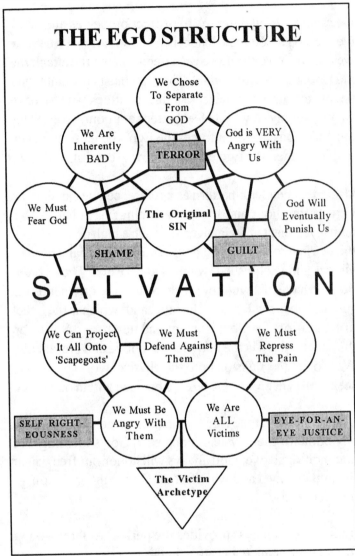

Fig. 6: The Structure of the Ego

we create strong defenses to protect ourselves and what we see as our complete innocence. At some level we know we are guilty, so the more we defend against the attack the more we reinforce our guilt. Thus, we must constantly find people to hate, to criticize, to judge, to attack, and to make wrong simply so we can feel better about ourselves. This dynamic constantly reinforces the Ego's belief system and, in this manner, the Ego ensures its own survival.

Using this behavior pattern as a reference, we can explain why, throughout history, human beings have had such a high investment in their anger and such a high need to break the world into victims and persecutors, villains and heroes, victors and vanquished, winners and losers. The perception we have of a we/they world reflects our own internal split between the Ego, on the one hand, which is the belief in separation, fear, punishment and death, and Spirit, on the other, which is the knowledge of love and eternal life. We project this division onto the physical world by always seeing the enemy as *out there*, rather than within ourselves.

Contrary to what the Ego would have us believe, we actually come to the physical plane with God's blessing and unconditional love. God always will honor our free will at the highest level and will offer no Divine intervention — unless asked.

Radical Forgiveness provides the perfect tool for asking for such assistance, because, in the process, you demonstrate to God that you have seen beyond the Ego and glimpsed the truth — that only love is real — and that we are One with God.

6: Hideouts and Scapegoats

Since undoing the twin psychological ego-defense mechanisms of repression and projection lies at the very core of Radical Forgiveness, a closer inspection of these mechanisms might be helpful. Operating together, repression and projection wreak havoc upon our relationships and our lives. Together they create and maintain the victim archetype. Understanding how they work enables us to counteract the Ego's use of them to keep us separated from each other and from God.

1. Repression

Operating as a normal psychological defense mechanism, repression occurs when feelings like terror, guilt or rage become so overwhelming that the mind simply blocks them from conscious awareness entirely. This makes repression a powerful mental safety device, for without this blocking mechanism we easily could go mad. It works so effectively that absolutely no memory of the feelings, or the event which precipitated them, remain — totally blocked out of conscious awareness for days, weeks or years — sometimes even forever.

Suppression:

Repression should not be confused with this other, similar but less severe, defense mechanism. Suppression occurs when we *consciously* refuse to acknowledge emotions that we do not want to feel or express. Though we know they are there, we try to push, or *stuff* them away and refuse to deal with them. However, continued denial of them for long periods of time may lead to a *numbness* equivalent to them becoming repressed.

Repressed Guilt and Shame

Guilt is a universal human experience. Deep in our unconscious mind we have such overwhelming, Ego induced, guilt and shame about the thought, albeit not true, that we separated from God (the original sin), that we have no choice but to repress this feeling. We absolutely could not handle these emotions otherwise.

Guilt and shame are different emotions. We feel guilt when we feel have *done* wrong. Shame takes us to a deeper level of guilt where we have a sense of actually *being* wrong. With shame, the Ego makes us feel inherently wrong at the very core of our being. No shame or guilt is as deep seated as the shame of the original sin, the central, but entirely false, plank of the Ego's belief system.

Shame Blocks Energy

Young children can be easily shamed, say, when they wet themselves, get an erection, show anger, act shy, and so on. While these may be natural occurrences, the children nevertheless feel the shame, and the cumulative effects of this feeling can become overwhelming. Consequently, they repress their shame, but it remains in the unconscious mind as well as in the body. It becomes locked into their system at the cellular level and becomes an energy block in the body. If left unresolved for too long, this block gives rise to either mental/emotional problems or physical problems or both. Repressed emotion now is recognized by many researchers to be one of the principal causes of cancer.

Repressed Feelings

A large trauma, such as the death of a parent, can cause a child to repress emotion. Likewise, something seemingly insignificant, such as casual critical remark interpreted as meaningful, or an event incorrectly assumed to be his fault, can cause emotions to be repressed. Children nearly always interpret a divorce as their fault, for example. Research suggests that children remember conversations their parents had while they were still in the womb. A discussion about an unwanted pregnancy before birth can lead to a child's feelings of being unwanted and fear of being abandoned. Such feelings would be repressed even at such an early time in the child's life.

Generational Guilt

Groups and even nationalities commonly repress accumulated generational guilt. Without doubt, this is the case now with black and white Americans over slavery. The racial problems we now experience in America all stem from the

79

unresolved and repressed guilt within white people and unresolved and repressed rage in the blacks.

The Dark Side

We also experience intense shame over aspects of ourselves that we dislike and, therefore, disown. Carl Jung,
the famous Swiss psychiatrist, referred to this as our
shadow, because it represents the dark side of ourselves,
the part that we do not want to see or to have seen. This
part of ourselves could kill another human being, knows
we could have taken part in the killing of six million Jews
had we been German during that time, knows we might
have owned and brutalized slaves had we been born white
in the South before the Civil War, could hurt or rape someone, is greedy or avaricious, is rageful and vengeful, or is
in some other way deviant or unacceptable. Any such characteristic of ourselves or area of our lives that brings us
feelings of shame, we classify as our shadow and then repress it.

Sitting On a Volcano

Repressing this kind of energy feels like sitting on a volcano! We never know when our strength will give out,
thus allowing the lava (shadow) to spurt forth and wreak
havoc on our world. This explains why we need to bring
in a scapegoat on whom we can project all that shame.
That way we can be free of it, at least temporarily.

2. Projection

Even when we have repressed the feelings and/or memories associated with a life event, we know, on an unconscious level, that the shame, guilt or self-criticism associated with it remains with us. So, we attempt to rid ourselves of that pain by *taking it out* of ourselves and transferring it on to someone, or something, else *outside* of ourselves. This projection process allows us to forget we ever possessed such feelings.

Once we project what we do not want to own onto someone else, we see them, rather than us, possessing those qualities. So, if we repress our guilt and then project it, we make that person the wrong one. If we repress our anger and then project it, we see them as the angry one. We can accuse them of all the things we feared we would be accused of ourselves. No wonder we feel so relieved when we project! In so doing, we make someone else responsible for everything terrible that happens to us or for what we see as negative about ourselves. Then, we can demand that they be punished, so we can feel even more righteous and safe from attack.

This explains why we love to watch the news on television. The news provides us with an opportunity to project all our guilt and shame on the murderers, rapists, corrupt politicians, and other *bad* people we see on the screen. After doing so, we can go to bed feeling okay about ourselves. The news, and all the other television programs that feature *bad* people and situations, endlessly provides us with convenient scapegoats upon whom to project.

81

Recognize When You're Projecting

As soon as you find yourself judging someone, you know you are projecting. Anger serves as the constant companion of projection, for the Ego uses this emotion in its attempt to justify the projection of guilt. Whenever you get angry, you also know you are projecting your own guilt onto others.

What you find so objectionable about another person simply serves as a reflection of that part of you that you have rejected and denied in yourself (your shadow) and projected onto them instead. If this was not so, you would not be upset.

This concept — *what we attack and judge in others is really what we condemn in ourselves* — is the central idea behind Radical Forgiveness and the key to our own soul-level healing.

Resonance

We feel victimized by other people precisely because they resonate with our own guilt, anger, fear, or rage. (See next chapter.) It feels like they are *doing something to us* to make us angry. When we own that the feelings begin with us, not with them, we can drop the need to feel victimized.

The Attack/Defense Cycle

Though repression and projection are meant as temporary relief valves for the psyche, the Ego co-opted them as the means to maintain itself. Remember, the Ego simply consists of a set of beliefs, the central one being that we are separate from God. Following from that belief comes the belief that God is after us and when he catches us he will punish us severely. The Ego uses the dynamics of repression and projection to hide these beliefs, as well as the guilt and fear that accompanies them, from our consciousness. Hence, repression and projection become a permanent way of being for us. Our whole life revolves around our continual repression, denial and projection, all of which are maintained in perpetuity by the never-ending fear/attack and defense/attack cycles. This provides a perfect recipe for continual internal conflict.

The Drive For Wholeness

In spite of the incredible efficiency of repression and projection, the innate drive for wholeness emanating from our souls possesses more power than the Ego. This drive for wholeness originates from that part of us that knows the truth and is not content to deny it and project it. This part, the soul, which is equivalent to "the still small voice" that cries out for love, carries the same energy that creates our opportunities for learning and for healing — the energy of Radical Forgiveness.

"A Course in Miracles" expresses the same idea. It says that, although all relationships have as their purpose the projection of guilt, relationships become 'holy' when their original purpose changes to forgiveness. Forgiveness leads to joining, while projections leads to separation. Thus, forgiveness undoes projection.

83

Fear Of Intimacy

Every person we meet offers us the opportunity to choose between projection or forgiveness, union or separation. However, the more intimate we become with someone and the closer they get to our true self, the more likely it becomes that they will learn the guilty truth about us. This possibility of being "discovered" creates enormous fear inside us, and the temptation to project becomes almost irresistible. At this point, fear of intimacy becomes so strong that most relationships fall apart.

The Purpose Of All Relationships

To move forward and succeed, we must understand this phenomena and use Radical Forgiveness to stay in the relationship and to fulfill its 'holy' purpose — which is to heal the people involved.

As we saw in Jill's Story, Radical Forgiveness can certainly save marriages! However, this is not necessarily the goal. If the purpose of the relationship has been fulfilled, which is to say that the people are healed, the relationship may need to dissolve naturally and peacefully.

7: Attraction & Resonance

As mentioned previously, we project our guilt and anger onto people who have the capacity to *resonate* with our feelings, and such people become convenient scapegoats.

Just as a radio station uses a certain frequency to broadcast its programs, so our emotions (energy in motion), vibrate at certain frequencies. People who resonate with our feelings vibrate at that same rate. Since they are already vibrating in a like manner, it becomes easy to project our own feelings onto them.

Our core beliefs also have a certain frequency. By speaking them aloud, we give our beliefs even more energy, and they take on a causal quality in the Universe. Thus, our spoken beliefs cause effects in our world. In addition, other people *resonate* with the energetic frequency of that belief. In other words, they vibrate sympathetically at the same rate with it. When they do so, they are attracted into our lives to mirror our beliefs back to us. That gives us a chance to look at and, if necessary, to change our minds about that belief. It is not only negative beliefs get mirrored back to us, either. For example, if we are loving and trusting, we will tend to attract people into our lives who are likewise trustworthy and nurturing.

Recall from Part 1 that my sister, Jill, had a belief that she would never be enough for any man. This belief resonated with a man who was a sexual addict. He provided the ideal partner for her, because he supported her belief by continually having sex with other women, thus showing her she was *not enough* for him. She did not make the connection in that relationship and, consequently, did not heal the pain that created this belief in the first place. So, she found another man (Jeff) who resonated with her belief. He supported her belief differently by using his own issue of co-dependence with his daughter, Lorraine, as the catalyst. In this situation, she saw the connection and realized that he was mirroring her belief that she was not enough, and both of them healed.

If you want to know what you dislike about yourself and have likely disowned, simply look at what annoys you about the people who come into your life. Look into the mirror they provide. If you seem to attract a lot of angry people into your life, you probably have not dealt with some anger of your own. If people seem to withhold love from you, some part of you is unwilling to give love. If people seem to steal things from you, part of you behaves dishonestly or feels dishonest. If people betray you, maybe you have betrayed someone in the past.

Look at the issues that upset you, too. If abortion really makes you mad, maybe a part of you shows little reverence for life in other ways, or a part of you knows it could abuse a child. If you are passionately against homosexuality, maybe you cannot accept the part of you that sometimes feels homosexually inclined.

Hall of Mirrors

The reflection does not always appear that readily or as simply. For example, sometimes we do not identify with the specific behavior as much as we do with the underlying meaning it holds for us. A man who gets angry about his wife's overeating and obesity may not be resonating with any personal tendency to overeat; instead, he might be resonating with her use of food to avoid dealing with emotional problems, because it mirrors his tendency to run away from his own emotional problems. Clearly, seeing what others mirror for us can become like looking at the myriad of distorted images in a hall of mirrors.

Automatic Reversal of Projection

The beauty of Radical Forgiveness lies in the fact that it does not require that we recognize what we project. We simply forgive the person for what is happening at the time. In doing so, we automatically undo the projection no matter how complicated the situation. The reason for this is simple: The person represents only the original pain that caused us to project in the first place. As we forgive him/her we clear that original pain. Moreover, no matter what we see as our problems, only one basic problem actually exists for any of us — our guilt about separating from God. All other problems derive from this original one.

Ironically, the people who seem to upset us the most are those who, at the soul level, love and support us the most. Almost always, and often at great expense to themselves in terms of their own discomfort, these individuals try to teach us something about ourselves and to encourage us to move towards healing. Remember, this is not a personality-to-personality exchange. In fact, more than likely the personalities of these individuals clash terribly. Instead, the souls of each player set up the scenario in the hope that the person eventually will see their issue and heal.

Don't Take Life So Personally

Who comes into our lives to help us accomplish this task is actually irrelevant. If one particular person does not take the job, somebody else will. The tragedy is that, as the victim, we seldom understand this. We imagine that we just happened to be the unlucky recipient of a particular person's harmful behavior. It does not occur to us that we might have (at the soul level) attracted the person and the situation to ourselves for a reason and that, had it not been this person, it simply would have been someone else. We mistakenly feel that but for this person we would not have had the problem. In other words, we see the problem as entirely with the other person, whom we now feel justified in hating and resenting for *causing* us pain and unhappiness.

Blaming Our Parents

We often hear this type of blame when people talk about their parents. "If I'd had different parents, I'd be whole and complete today," people say. Wrong. They could have chosen a different set of parents, that's true, but the new set would have given them the exact same experience, because that's what their soul wanted.

Repeating Relationship Patterns

When we see ourselves as victims, we think only about killing the messenger. We miss the message. This explains why people today go from marriage to marriage recreating the same relationship dynamic each time. They do not get the message with the first spouse, so they go on to another who continues trying to relay the message the last spouse tried to relay.

Co-dependency And Mutual Projection

We also find others onto whom we project our own self-hatred who will not only accept it but reciprocate by projecting theirs back onto us. We call this kind of agreement a co-dependent or addictive relationship. That special someone compensates for what we feel is missing in ourselves by continually telling us we are okay, so we avoid feeling our shame about who we are. We do the same thing for them in return, thus both people learn to manipulate each other with highly conditional love based on the underlying guilt. (The stereotypical Jewish Mother is a wonderful example of this archetype.) The moment the other person withdraws approval, we are forced to confront our guilt and self-hatred again, and everything collapses. Love turns immediately into hate, and each partner attacks the other. This explains why we see so many faltering relationships turn into a cauldron of hate virtually in an instant.

89

8: Cause & Effect

Central to the concept of Radical Forgiveness is the Law of Cause and Effect, which states that every action has an equal reaction. Therefore, every cause must have an effect, and every effect must have a cause. Since thoughts are causal in nature, every thought has an effect in the world. In other words, we — unconsciously for the most part — create our world with our thoughts.

When we vibrate at a high frequency, such as when we pray, meditate or contemplate, we can create consciously and intentionally through thought. Most of the time, however, we do so quite unconsciously. Individual random thoughts do not carry a lot of energy, so they possess a relatively small effect. However, thoughts accompanied by larger amounts of energy, especially emotional or creative energy, have a much larger effect in the world. Thus, they play a larger hand in creating our reality.

When a thought gathers sufficient energy to become a belief, it has an even greater effect in the world. It becomes an operating principle in our lives, and we then create effects — circumstances, situations, even physical events that hold true to that belief. What we believe about the world is how it always will be for us.

Acceptance of the principle that thought is creative is fundamental to understanding of Radical Forgiveness, for it allows us to see that what turns up in our lives represents what we have created with our thoughts and our beliefs. It allows us to see that we simply are projecting all our thoughts and beliefs about *the way things are* onto the world.

Projecting the Illusion

Metaphorically, we run a movie, called ***Reality***, through our mind (the projector), and we project it *out there*.

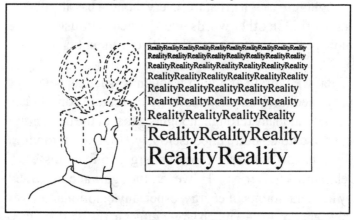

Fig. 7: Projecting Our Own Reality

Once we understand that what we call reality is just our projections, instead of blaming others we can begin to take responsibility for what we have created with our thoughts. When we change our perception and drop our attachment to our belief that what appears on the screen represents reality, we experience Radical Forgiveness.

Consciousness Determines What Happens

While it may seem difficult to see the principle of cause and effect operating in our lives, it becomes apparent when we trace back from what is occurring. In other words, if you want to know your beliefs, just look at what is happening. That will tell you what you are projecting. For example, if you keep getting attacked or disasters keep happening to you, the likelihood is that you believe the world is inherently an unsafe place. You are creating these events to prove that you are right about that and people are supporting you in this belief by appearing to you to behave in a threatening or dangerous manner.

Some friends of mine have a spiritual conference center in the mountains of North Carolina. Werner, being of a prudent nature, thought he and his wife, Jean, should have insurance to protect their buildings against fire, storm damage and the frequent tornadoes that come through each season. Jean was very much against the idea. She felt having such insurance would clearly indicate to the Universe that they did not trust in their safety. Now, I am not advocating this, but they decided against purchasing the insurance.

The following year, a huge storm hit their very mountain and devastated the area. Thousands of trees were uprooted and thrown down. When my wife and I drove up to visit them two weeks later, we couldn't believe our eyes. It looked like a war zone. They had obviously been obliged to cut their way out. The storm had happened while 36 people were at the center attending a conference, and they

93

were unable to leave for two whole days. However, in spite of all the trees down, not one car nor any of the buildings were touched — and both were right in amongst the trees. Trees fell within inches of structures and autos but miraculously damaged nothing. For my friends, it was a great confirmation of their faith and willingness to trust.

Looking at this from a cause and effect standpoint, Jean recognized that buying insurance reinforced a belief (a cause) in adversity and would create the energy for something bad (an effect) to happen. Instead she chose the thought (cause) "We are doing God's work here, and we are totally safe." The effect, as it played out in the world (reality), was that in the midst of chaos nothing bad happened.

As I have said, if you want to know your beliefs, look at what you have in your life — or what you do not have in your life. If, for example, you do not have love in your life and do not seem to be able to create a loving relationship, examine your beliefs about self-worthiness, or about safety with the opposite sex. Of course, this may not be as easy as it sounds, for the beliefs you hold may be buried deep in your subconscious mind.

You Don't Need To Know Why?

The good news is that you do not have to know why you created your situation or what beliefs led you to its creation. Just seeing the situation's existence as an opportunity to perceive it differently — *being willing* to see it as perfect — is enough to bring about the required shift in perception and a healing of the original pain.

The truth is that, from the World of Humanity, we cannot know *why* a situation is as it is, because the answer lies in the world of Divine Truth, and we can know little to nothing of that world as long as we are in human form. *All we can do is surrender to the situation.*

Just Surrender

If new insights, connections, old memories, emotional movements, and other psychic events are necessary for the desired change to occur, they will happen automatically and without our conscious control. If we try to figure it all out and manipulate the unfolding process, this creates resistance and blocks the process completely, which places us right back in the path of the Ego.

Men tend to have more difficulty with surrendering than women. This is because male energy is taking action, controlling, figuring things out, and making things work. For men to move up the vibrational scale and live more in the spiritual realm of surrender and acceptance, they must be willing to access more of the female energy within them. Otherwise, they will remain stuck in the world of illusion and under the control of the Ego, separated from God and their true nature. This is the challenge that men face in the Aquarian Age.

9: Mission "Forgiveness"

Nnone of us can return home to God until we (as an entire species) have completed the mission we created for ourselves, which is to transcend the Ego (prove untrue our belief in our separation from God) and transform the energies of fear, death and duality. This is our collective mission. Each of us serves as an individual expression of that mission, and the life we create for ourselves here in the World of Humanity purely serves that purpose.

Our Individual Mission

To transform energies we must experience them totally, working through them and *forgiving* them, which means seeing the perfection in them. The decision about which energies we work with is not decided by us at the human level. That decision pre-dates our incarnation and is made by our soul group — a group to which we belong made up of souls who either incarnate with us or act as our spirit guides during our incarnation.

Once it is decided which energies we shall work with, we then carefully choose parents who will provide the experiences we need as children and arrange for others to come along at the right time to play their respective roles in the

other experiences necessary to the accomplishm
mission. We then create dramas throughout ou
lives that allow us to experience the feelings o
that make up our mission. These dramas serve
tunities for us to see the illusion, forgive, heal,
doing, remember who we are.

Mission Amnesia

Seen from the World of Divine Truth prior to incarnation,
the mission seems easy. However, once we incarnate it
takes on a new level of difficulty. This is due not only to
the greater density of energy in the World of Humanity but
because the mission must be undertaken free of any awareness that we have chosen this experience. If we knew
(remembered) the truth about our purpose, the experience
would be senseless. How can we remember who we are
if we have never forgotten? So, Spirit creates the human
experience in such a way that when we are born into our
bodies we lose all recall of our mission and all awareness
that life on the physical plane is, in fact, *a setup*.

To accomplish our mission (to transform energies) we must
have a total experience of those energies. For example, to
transform the energy of *victim*, we must feel totally victimized. To transform the energy of fear, we must feel ter-
rorized. To transform the energy of hate, we must be con-
sumed with hatred. In other words, we must go fully into
the experience of being human. It is only when we have
fully felt the emotions connected with these energies that
we gain the ability to move into the full forgiveness of them.
And, it is in forgiving them that we remember who we are.

From this viewpoint, clearly we are never in a position to judge anyone. A person who appears hateful may have chosen to transform that energy as his mission. Thus, his hateful behavior, even though it seems to harm others *(who may have volunteered to have hate projected at them as their mission)*, is neither right nor wrong. His hateful behavior simply represents what needs to happen to transform the energy of hate. Period.

The energy of hate is transformed when someone who feels hated sees the love beneath the hate and forgives the person for hating him. In that moment, hearts open and love flows between the two people. Thus, hate is transformed into love.

Janet's Story

Janet, who had cancer, attended one of my early cancer retreats, but her tumor was not the only thing eating away at her. The anger she felt concerning her 23-year-old daughter, Melanie, was doing the same.

By all accounts, Melanie exhibited some pretty strong rebellious behavior. She was verbally abusive to Janet and her new husband, Jim, and she had attached herself to a rather unsavory man. "I hate her with a vengeance," Janet related. "Her behavior towards me and Jim is simply abominable, and I can't stand it any more. I really hate her."

We dug a little deeper into Janet's personal history and found that a similar relationship had existed between Janet and her own mother. It was not as clear and dramatic as

99

the drama with Melanie, but the dynamic was similar. Janet had resented how much her mother controlled her and tried to run her life. Janet did not rebel like Melanie, though. Instead, she became withdrawn and cold toward her mother.

We began to explore how the dynamic with Melanie reflected her soul's willingness to help her heal her issues with her mother, but Janet was not willing to see this. She simply was too angry to hear anything that did not correspond with her feelings. So, we asked her to move into her anger, to feel and to express it by beating cushions with a tennis racquet and shouting. (Anger is very effectively released through the combination of physical action and the use of the voice.) Although she released some anger toward her mother, her anger with Melanie remained.

Janet's *Satori*

That evening's retreat session was reserved for **Satori-Breath.** To experience Satori-Breath and use it for healing, everyone in the group lies on the floor and breathes consciously and vigorously for about an hour while listening to loud music. (See Part 4, Chapter 26.) While this may sound bizarre, breathing in this manner often results in emotional release, insight and integration of change at the cellular level. That night, Janet gave credence to the name *Satori,* which means *enlightenment.*

After the breathing session, people began sharing what had happened for them during the exercise. As soon as Janet began to share, we knew something important had happened.

Her voice was soft and sweet, whereas before it had been hard and abrasive. Her posture was relaxed and open, whereas before it had been tight and constricted. There was not a trace of the anger that had filled her being and which we all had felt emanating from her previously. She was calm and evidently peaceful. In fact, she hardly seemed the same person.

"I have no idea what all this means," she began. *"All I know is that I saw something while I was breathing, and it felt more real than anything I can possibly describe. Nothing much happened for quite a while after I began breathing,"* she continued. *"Then, suddenly I found myself floating in space, out there in the ethers. I was not in a body, and I knew with certainty that I was re-experiencing a time before I came into my current life. I was pure spirit. I have never felt so peaceful and calm. Then, I became aware of Melanie, also in spirit form. She came close, and we began to dance together — just dancing in space without limitation.*

"We began a conversation about coming into our next lifetime together," Janet said. *"This lifetime. The big question we had to decide was who would play what role — who was going to play the mother and who was going to play the daughter. It didn't much matter, for either way it was going to be a difficult assignment for us both. It would be a very strong test of our love. We had to decide, so we agreed that I would be the mother and she would be the daughter, and that we would incarnate soon thereafter. That's about it,"* she concluded.

101

"It doesn't sound like a whole lot happened, but really it did. I just can't put it into words. I just can't describe the depth and the meaning of what I experienced."

Energies Transformed

We discussed her experience and looked at the ideas of reincarnation, karma and mission as suggested by Janet's vision. Several others in the group felt strongly about her experience and saw parallels in their own lives. I suggested that Janet say nothing at all to Melanie when she returned home after the retreat. Within a few days of Janet's homecoming, Melanie called her mother and asked if she could come and talk. Janet agreed, and, while the first meeting was tentative and awkward, their relationship changed dramatically after that. Melanie soon dropped all her bizarre behavior, sent the unsavory boyfriend packing and came home to be with her mother and to take care of her during her illness. They literally became best friends and were quite inseparable after that. In addition, Janet's Mother began calling more often, and gradually their relationship began to improve as well.

In this example, the transformation of energy happened in a roundabout way. Janet was extremely resistant to forgiving Melanie. Her soul guided her to the retreat so she could do a process that opened her to a remembrance of her mission agreement, which, in turn, enabled her to see the perfection in the situation. By forgiving Melanie she transformed the hate in their relationship and, as a result, healed the original pain between herself and her mother.

10: Transforming The Victim Archetype

As we saw in the last chapter, our primary mission is to transform the victim archetype and raise the consciousness of the planet. But what does it mean to transform anything, and how does it raise consciousness?

The first thing to understand is that we can transform something only when we choose it as our spiritual mission. We make the decision about our mission not in this world but in the World of Divine Truth prior to reincarnating. This *contract* is held in the eighth chakra located about ten inches above the crown chakra.

The second thing to realize is that transforming something *does not* mean changing it. In fact:

> *To transform anything we must experience it*
> *fully and love it just the way it is.*

For example, maybe your individual mission involved being born into an abusive family to experience the abuse first hand and to know it either as a victim or as a perpetrator. Remember, once you incarnate, your memory of your agreed-upon mission disappears. If you remembered your mission, you would not experience the energy and the feelings of victimhood as fully. Only in the experience of being victimized can you possibly come to realize what lies behind the illusion of victimhood — the projection of your guilt. If you are able to look beyond the illusion of the perpetrator and recognize these actions as a call for love, and if you respond with love and total acceptance, the victim energy is transformed and the consciousness of all involved is raised. In addition, the energy that holds the pattern of abuse disappears and the behavior stops immediately. That is what transformation is all about.

On the other hand, if we do not recognize the truth in the situation, or do not see beyond the illusion, and we try to change the physical circumstances, we lock up the energy that holds the pattern of abuse in place and nothing changes. That means we will have failed in our mission. That is OK of course. We are expected to fail many times. When we do, we just reincarnate again and again until we get it right.

Only Love Transforms

Only love has the ability to transform energies like child abuse, corporate greed, murder and all other so-called evils of the world. Nothing else has any impact. Actions taken to change such situations, such as removing a child from an abusive environment, while humane in and of themselves, do not create transformation. The reason for this is simple: First, such action arises from fear, not love. Second, our intervention and our judgments maintain the energy pattern of abuse and lock them up more securely.

This explains why the decision to transform something can

be made only from the World of Divine Truth. We humans are so locked into our beliefs about pain and suffering, fear and death, that, even while we may believe that a particular child's soul came into this world to experience abuse and actually wants to feel abused, we simply cannot stand by and watch this happen. While the mission looks easy from the world of Divine Truth, it appears quite different down here on the physical plane. Who could possibly leave an abused child in an abusive environment? We cannot help but intervene. We are human!

Radical Forgiveness Transforms

As humans, we are still not totally impotent in this regard, because we can transform the energy of something like child abuse by using Radical Forgiveness. If we truly forgive, in the radical sense, all those involved in the abusive situation, we definitely have an impact on the energy pattern. Ultimately, the child will have to forgive to finally change the pattern, but each time any of us, in any situation, whether we are personally involved or not, choose to see the perfection in the situation, we change the energy. If we all sat and watched the news from that perspective, seeing through the illusions being presented and surrendering to the inherent perfection of the Divine Plan unfolding, the world would be different immediately.

Nelson Mandela Has Shown Us How

How Nelson Mandela handled the South African situation when apartheid finally ended in the early 1990s, is an object lesson in Radical Forgiveness. Apartheid, the white

105

dominated political system in place for three-quarters of a century, kept blacks and whites separated — the whites in luxury and the blacks in terrible poverty. Mandela himself was imprisoned for 26 years. Upon his release he became President of the country. South Africa was ripe for a bloodbath of revenge, yet Mandela brought about an amazingly peaceful transition — the hallmark of which was not revenge but forgiveness.

It was not so much what he did that prevented the predicted bloodbath from occurring, but how he handled the energy. He refused to take revenge, and, on behalf of all the people, he transcended the victim archetype. This, in turn, collapsed the energy pattern of potential violence already in place and waiting to be triggered. South Africa remains in transition today and not without problems, but its progress is far more than we could have dreamed possible a few decades ago.

Our collective mission to transform the victim archetype demands that we all follow Mandela's lead and move beyond the experience of victimhood. If we do not, we will stay hopelessly addicted to our woundedness and to the victim archetype.

Spirit Nudges

Deep inside our subconscious mind, we are in touch with our mission. Spirit keeps presenting opportunities to transform the victim energy by bringing things like incest, child abuse, sexual abuse, and racial hatred to the surface. Each one of us can embrace this mission by practicing Radical Forgiveness in any of these situations. If taken by enough of us, that shift in perception that allows us to see the perfection will transform the situation so the need for such energy patterns disappears.

Exercise in Transformation

To transform the victim archetype, practice the following: Every time you watch the news, shift your consciousness from one of judgment to one of seeing the perfection in the situation. Instead of accepting at face value a story about racial prejudice, for example, help transform the energy of racial disharmony. Do so by looking at the person or situation that would ordinarily receive your judgment and censure and seeing if you can move into a space of loving acceptance. Know that the people in the story are living out their part in the Divine plan. Do not see anyone as a victim and refuse to label anyone as a villain. People are just acting in dramas being played out so healing can occur. *Remember, God does not make mistakes!*

11: The Ego Fights Back

By reminding us that we are spiritual beings having a human experience, Radical Forgiveness raises our vibration and moves us in the direction of spiritual evolution.

Such growth represents a real threat to the Ego, because the more spiritually evolved we become, the more likely it will be that we will remember who we are — and that we are one with God. Once we have this realization, we have no more need for the Ego.

The more we use Radical Forgiveness therefore, the more the Ego fights back and tries to seduce us into remaining addicted to the victim archetype. One way it accomplishes this task is by using our own tools of spiritual growth. A good example of this is found in the Ego's use of *inner child work* to meet its own ends.

Inner child work gives us a way to look within ourselves and to heal the wounds of childhood we still carry within us as adults and that continue to effect our lives today. However, the Ego sees an opportunity for its own survival in our focus on our woundedness. It uses this phenomenon to strengthen our addiction to the victim archetype. After all, what is the inner child but a metaphor for our woundedness and our addiction to the pain that it holds captive within us? Such addiction is characterized by the constant revisiting of our wounds, giving them power through constantly speaking about them and using them as the means to finding intimacy.

Blaming Our Parents

Much of the inner child work of the eighties focused heavily on blaming our parents, or someone else, for the fact that we are unhappy now. The idea "I would be happy today if it weren't for my parents," is the mantra associated with this work. It gives us permission to feel that "they did this to us," a perception that is much easier to live with than believing we have somehow *requested* to be treated in this manner. Such a viewpoint also pleases the Ego, because it automatically recreates us as victim. As long as we continue blaming our parents for our problems, each succeeding generation continues this belief pattern.

Clearing Emotional Toxicity

I do not wish to imply that getting in touch with our repressed childhood rage and pain and finding ways to release it, is bad. In fact, doing so is essential. We must first do this work before moving onto forgiveness, for we cannot forgive if we are angry. However, too many workshops and therapies focus purely on our anger and fail to help us transform it through forgiveness of any kind. When we couple anger work with Radical Forgiveness, all sorts of repressed emotional and mental toxicity are cleared and the permanent release of anger becomes possible. Thus, we move out of woundedness and beyond victimhood.

Navaho Forgiveness Ritual

I once heard Caroline Myss describe the ritual that the Navaho Indians had for preventing woundology from becoming an addictive pattern. While they certainly recognized the need for people to speak of their wounds and to have them *witnessed* by the group, they understood that speaking about their wounds gave them power, especially when done to excess. Therefore, if a person had a wound or a grievance to share, the tribe would meet and the person could bring it to the circle. This person was allowed to air his grievance three times and everyone listened with empathy and compassion. On the fourth occasion, however, as the person came into the circle, everyone turned their backs. "Enough! We have heard you express your concern three times. We have received it. Now let it go. We will not hear it again," they said. This served as a powerful ritual of support for letting go of past pain.

Imagine if we were to support our friends in that same manner? What if, after they had complained about their wounds and their victimization three times, we then said, "I have heard you enough on this subject. It's time you let it go. I will not give your wounds power over you any longer by allowing you to talk about them to me. I love you too much."

I am sure if we did this, our friends would call us traitors. They would see our behavior not as an act of pure loving

111

support but of betrayal and would likely turn against us in
an instant.

Being a True Friend

If we are to truly support each other in the journey of spiritual evolution, I believe we have no choice but to take the
risk, draw a line in the sand with those we love and do our
best to help move them beyond their addiction to their
wounds. Such action will lead us to the achievement of
our collective mission to transform the victim archetype
and to remember who we really are.

Note: In Part 4, a ritual guided meditation is offered in
which the wounded inner child is released and allowed to
make its transition back to the world of Divine Truth.
(Chapter 22)

12: Time, Medicine & Forgiveness

Our spiritual evolution brings with it a new appreciation for and knowledge of our physical bodies and how to care for them. The medical paradigm we have held for the last 300 years — ever since the French philosopher, Rene Descartes defined the body as a machine — is changing radically as it moves towards a holistic, mind-body approach.

We used to think of health as the absence of disease. Now, we think of health in terms of how well our *life force* (prana, chi, etc), flows through our bodies. For optimum health, this life-force must be able to flow freely. We cannot be healthy if our bodies are clogged with the energy of resentment, anger, sadness, guilt, and grief.

When we speak here of the body, we include not only the physical body, which is also an *energy body*, but the subtle bodies which surround us as well. These we refer to individually as the etheric body, the emotional body, the mental body, and the causal body. They each have a different frequency. Whereas we used to define our body in terms of chemicals and molecules, physicists have taught us how to see them as *dense condensations of interacting energy patterns.*

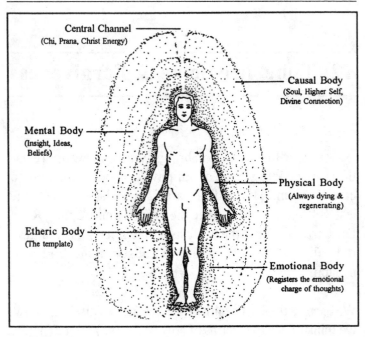

Central Channel
(Chi, Prana, Christ Energy)

Causal Body
(Soul, Higher Self,
Divine Connection)

Mental Body
(Insight, Ideas,
Beliefs)

Physical Body
(Always dying &
regenerating)

Etheric Body
(The template)

Emotional Body
(Registers the emotional
charge of thoughts)

Fig. 8: The Subtle Energy Bodies

The subtle fields envelop the physical body in layers like vibrating sheaths of energy, each one an octave higher than the other. However, they are not fixed bands with clear boundaries as shown in the diagram above. Rather, they are, to a large degree, diffused within the same space as if they were all part of an ocean of energy surrounding our bodies. The subtle bodies are not so much defined by their position in space as by the different frequencies at which they vibrate.

The subtle bodies resonate harmonically with the vibrating patterns of the physical body, enabling consciousness (mind) to interact with the body. This is what we mean when we speak of the *body-mind continuum,* with mind existing both inside and outside the physical body. (For more details on the qualities and purpose ascribed to each of these subtle bodies, refer to Part 3, Chapter 14)

Clogged Filters Stress the Furnace

To ground this concept in a practical analogy, think of our bodies as being like the filters typically found in home heating furnaces — the kind we have to clean from time to time to ensure the furnace works efficiently. Just as these filters were designed to allow air to move easily through them, the same is true of our bodies. Life force must be free to flow easily through all our bodies — our physical body and our subtle bodies, too.

Whenever we judge, make someone wrong, blame, project, repress anger, hold resentment, etc., we create an energy block in our body(s). Each time we do this, our filter becomes a little more blocked and less energy remains available for our *furnace.* Sooner or later the filter fails and, starved of the vital oxygen it must have to keep burning, the *flame* dies. More simply, when our physical and subtle bodies become too clogged for life force to flow through easily, our body starts shutting down. In many cases, this manifests first as depression. Eventually, our body gets sick, and, if the blocks are not removed, we may die.

You may recall how my sister Jill felt a release of energy when she moved into Radical Forgiveness. Her life-force filter was blocked by her toxic belief system about her own

115

lack of worthiness, not to mention past resentments, anger, sadness, and frustrations over her current situation. When she let all that go, her energy blocks were cleared, which allowed her to shift her emotional state as well. Whenever you forgive radically, you release enormous amounts of life-force energy that then can be made available for healing, creativity and expressing your true purpose in life.

Farra's Flu Release

My good friend Farra Allen, co-founder of the Atlanta School of Massage and a mind-body counselor, took ill with a particularly virulent strain of flu that typically kept people in bed for 10 days or more. It hit him hard, but instead of giving all his power to the virus, he decided to do some inner work around it, work that might shift the energy pattern holding the virus in place. Using a process known as *active imagination*, which simply involves writing down thoughts as a *stream of consciousness*, he came upon a hitherto unconscious and unresolved emotional issue. He used Radical Forgiveness to clear the issue, and the flu disappeared almost immediately. He was working full-time and feeling great within two days of the onset of his illness. This was a powerful demonstration of the medicinal power of Radical Forgiveness.

Will Cancer Respond Too?

Suppose the illness had been cancer rather than the flu and it was our belief that it started as a deeply-repressed emotion. Thinking the cure lay in releasing that energy block, our recommendation might have been that my friend get in touch with the repressed feelings, feel them fully and then let them go.

However, unlike Farra's flu attack, which probably moved from his subtle body into his physical body in just a few days, this energy pattern might have taken many years to move from the subtle body into the physical body and, in time, to manifest as a disease. The question that haunts us then becomes, *'How long will it take for the disease process to fully reverse itself using emotional release work alone?'* Conceivably, it could require the same number of years it took for the disease to manifest — not very practical if you have cancer or some other disease where time is of the essence — or so it might seem, anyway.

Time Is a Factor In Healing

We used to think of time as something fixed and linear until Einstein proved that time actually is relative and that consciousness becomes a factor in the equation. The more elevated our consciousness, the faster we evolve and the faster things happen with regard to change in any physical matter to which we give attention.

Think of consciousness as our vibratory rate. It would probably take far too long to reverse the disease process of cancer energetically if we possess a low vibratory rate. It automatically will be low if we are in fear, hold anger and resentment in our beingness, think of ourselves as a victim, and/or have our energy locked up in the past. For the majority of us, this represents our consciousness most of

117

the time. Therefore, few of us could reverse a disease like cancer fast enough relying solely on releasing the emotional cause of the disease — that is, unless we found a way to raise our vibratory rate.

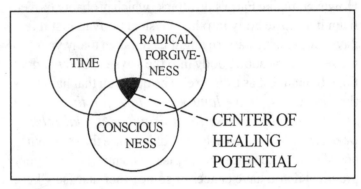

Fig. 9: Time & Healing.

By letting go of the victim archetype and bringing our energy into present time through the process of Radical Forgiveness, we might raise our vibration enough to create at least a quicker, if not immediate, disease reversal. We improve our chances if we also incorporate other ways of raising our vibration, such as prayer and meditation.

Example: A lady who attended one of our retreats had had several surgeries for ovarian cancer and had just been given by her doctors, at most, three months to live. She was depressed and had little life-force left. She said she only really came to the retreat because the people in her church had collected the money for her to come, so she felt obliged to do so. We worked with her and on the third day had a wonderful breakthrough that put her in touch with an event that occurred when she was 2 1/2 years old and had made her believe herself to be utterly worthless. She released a lot of emotion around that issue and grieved for the countless number of times she had created her life in ways that proved her worthless. After that, her life-force energy increased. By the time she left she was all fired up to find an alternative program that would help her beat the cancer and the doctor's prognosis. She was even willing to travel outside the USA if the method she chose was illegal in this country. (Many are illegal in the USA.) After two weeks of frantically searching for the treatment to which she felt most drawn, she suddenly realized that her healing would come through prayer. So, she went away to a place in up-state New York and worked with a couple who offered prayer-weeks. She literally prayed for a week. Upon her return, she went to her oncologist who examined her and said, "I don't know how to explain this, but you have absolutely no cancer in your body. I could say it was a spontaneous remission, but I believe in God and I am not willing to describe it in any other way than as a miracle."

This woman serves as a wonderful example of how raising the vibration through prayer reversed the physical condition in days rather than years. I believe that Radical Forgiveness would have done the same.

Seattle Forgiveness Study

An interesting, but as yet unpublished, study on forgiveness and time was conducted at Seattle University in CA. It involved a series of interviews with people who, by their own assessment, had been victimized. The researchers wanted to see how that perception changed over time. Preliminary findings showed that serenity, which was described as "having no resentment left," came NOT through any act of forgiveness but as a sudden *discovery* that they had forgiven. All reported that the more they tried to forgive, the harder it became and the more resentment they felt. They stopped trying to forgive and *just let go.* After varying intervals of time came the surprising realization that they no longer harbored resentment and that they had, in fact, forgiven. A later, and even more interesting, discovery revealed that the realization that they had forgiven was preceded by being forgiven themselves. (Who forgave them and for what was irrelevant.)

This study not only reinforces the insight that forgiveness cannot be willed but also shows that forgiveness happens as an internal transformation through a combination of surrendering one's attachment to resentment and accepting forgiveness for oneself.

Additionally, this study's results underscore the value of Step Nine in the Twelve-Step process used successfully by millions of people in Alcoholics Anonymous and other similar programs. Step Nine asks that we seek to make amends with those we have harmed and that we ask those people for forgiveness. When we find that we have in fact been forgiven, this frees our own energy to forgive not only others but ourselves as well.

Mock Forgiveness Only

Some might argue that the Seattle study illustrates the slowness of the forgiveness process and shows that forgiveness would offer a rather ineffective method for curing a disease such as cancer. In many cases, it took people decades to discover they had forgiven.

The important distinction to make, however, is that the study did not distinguish between Radical Forgiveness and Mock Forgiveness. What it described was definitely Mock Forgiveness. I would be willing to wager that, if the subject group had been divided into two — one group with insight into Radical Forgiveness and the other left basically to use Mock Forgiveness, the group with the additional insight would have reached the serenity state infinitely more quickly than the other group.

I am not claiming that Radical Forgiveness always occurs instantaneously either. Neither can it be claimed as a definitive *cure* for cancer. However, it certainly should be an integral part of any treatment protocol. I often go as far as to suggest that someone might delay serious medical treatment until they see if Radical Forgiveness creates enough of an effect to make such drastic intervention unnecessary. I would not suggest that with Mock Forgiveness.

Mary's Story

My friend Mary Pratt, a co-facilitator at many of my retreats denied for months that something was terribly wrong with her health. When she could not ignore the obvious any longer, she went to a doctor who told her she had stage three colon cancer. They wanted to operate immediately. She asked them for 30 days, and they reluctantly agreed. She went to a little cabin in the mountains and stayed there for a week, meditating and working on forgiving all the people in her life, including herself, using Radical Forgiveness. She fasted, prayed, cried, and literally went through *the dark night of the soul*. She came back home and worked with several practitioners to cleanse her body and strengthen her immune system. At the end of the 30-day period, the surgery was performed. Afterwards, the doctor wanted to know what she had done, for the cancer had all but disappeared and instead of the radical surgery they had said would be necessary, removal of the cancer required only minor intervention. That was five years, ago and she is now entirely cancer free.

Buying Time

In cases where the disease is so advanced or aggressive as to require immediate medical intervention, surgery, chemotherapy or radiation buys time. In that sense, such treatment becomes not only helpful but, at times, necessary.

Remember, there is no cure for cancer. Consequently, no matter what the medical treatment, the doctor's have an unspoken expectation that a recurrence is almost a forgone conclusion and just a question of time. I prefer to look at the treatment, assuming the patient survives it, as a way to buy the time to do the Radical Forgiveness work that could actually prevent any recurrence.

Preventive Medicine

Radical Forgiveness provides one of the best preventive medicines available. RFT, which I created for this purpose, clears the energy in the subtle bodies long before it becomes a block in the physical body. When I help people resolve forgiveness issues by using RFT, like I did with my sister Jill, I believe I am not only helping them heal a wound in their subtle body, I am helping them prevent disease occurring in the physical body. I am convinced that if we keep the energy flowing in our bodies as it was designed to do, we never will get sick.

Of course, adequate exercise, good diet and other such common sense practices help in this regard as well. However, keeping our energy bodies clear of emotional dross and toxicity is of primary importance to good health and healing. Unfortunately, this aspect of healing gets the least media attention despite the fact that, in America alone, one out of every five people take an anti-depressant drug like Prozac. Bearing in mind that depression always precedes cancer, we have to wonder whether is it mere coincidence that one out of five Americans also die of cancer.

Forgiveness And Cancer

I am often asked why I work with people who have cancer. I have had no personal experience with it, and I knew little about it from a medical standpoint when I began offering five-day cancer retreats for emotional and spiritual healing about five years ago.

123

It was only after doing this for some time that I realized why I was attracted to this work. It was because it linked up with my interest with forgiveness. That insight occurred when I discovered that nearly all cancer patients, besides having a lifetime habit of suppressing and repressing emotions, are known to share a marked inability to forgive.

I now believe that lack of forgiveness contributes to, and may even be a principal cause of, most cancers. Therefore, my healing work with cancer patients, and with those who want to prevent the disease from arising or reoccurring in their bodies, now centers almost entirely on RFT.

Jane's Story

Jane came to one of our five-day retreats in the North Georgia mountains. She had had a mastectomy and was awaiting a bone-marrow transplant. After the retreat, she came to me once a week for hypnotherapy and individual counseling. On the second visit she arrived in a distressed state, because a routine Magnetic Resonance Imaging (MRI) scan had that day discovered minute spots of cancer in her brain. While this new cancer was upsetting enough by itself, its appearance also was liable to spoil her chances of a transplant. The doctors planned to give her chemotherapy to try and arrest the cancer's progress. However, they were surprised at her condition, because normally metastasis proceeds from the breast to the liver and then to the brain. Very rarely does cancer proceed directly from the breast to the brain. To me, this seemed worthy of some exploration.

Jane, an attractive woman in her early forties, had not been involved in a romantic relationship for about seven years. She had a boyfriend of sorts, but she described the relationship as not much more than a close friendship. In fact, she said she looked upon him as her *buddy,* even though she had sex with him from time to time. As I probed further into her relationship situation, she got in touch with some incredible grief she still felt around a relationship she had ended a number of years ago. This eight-year relationship was extremely passionate and intense, and Jane clearly worshipped the man. Four years into this relationship, which she believed was soon to be consummated in marriage, she discovered that he was married already and had children. He had no intention of leaving his wife. Jane was devastated but could not stop seeing him. It took her another four extremely painful years to extricate herself from this relationship.

It was clear to me that, as a result of this failed relationship, Jane had shut down her emotions completely and would no longer allow herself to get involved so deeply with a man. Neither was I surprised that she had suffered a broken heart; most women with breast cancer have a broken heart somewhere in their history. (The breast is the organ of nurturance and is in the proximity of, and related to the heart.)

As she was going out the door at the end of our session, Jane said in a whisper, "I put him in the attic."

I stopped in my tracks. "What do you mean?" I asked.

"Well, everything I had accumulated over the years that had any connection to this man, or that would remind me of him, I stuffed in a box. I then put the box up in the attic. It's still there. I haven't touched it since."

I told her to sit down and tell me that again. I had her repeat the same thing three times. Suddenly, she saw the connection between the box in the attic that represented her broken love affair and her brain cancer. "Oh, my God," she said slowly. "That's him in my head, isn't it? He's in my attic."

I told her to go home, go up into the attic and take down the box. I told her to bring it with her to her next session, and we would go through it piece by piece. We planned for her to tell me the story around each item until we had exorcised his energy and released the pain that she had repressed. Jane understood that this might be the key to her healing and was very excited. Tragically, she had a seizure the next day and was taken back to the hospital. She died a month later without ever touching the box in the attic. Looking at the boxes contents and feeling the pain of her lost love may have been just too much for her to bear, and I feel, at some level, she may have decided to let go of life rather than face the pain.

Origins Of Illness

Energy blocks always begin in the subtle bodies first. Then, if they are not released at that level, they move into the physical body and ultimately manifest as diseases such as cancer, multiple sclerosis, diabetes, and the like. Thus, we can say that illness always begins in the subtle bodies first and moves inward.

We used to think that the best way to stay ahead of disease was to visit a medical doctor for a regular checkup. We now know that we are much better off having a consultation with someone who can read our aura — meaning that they can tune into the energy patterns of our subtle bodies, particularly the etheric body. They can see blocks building energetically long before they show up in the physical body. Medical intuitives can do the same.

There are now also sophisticated technological diagnostic systems that do this. They are mostly used by naturopaths, homeopaths, osteopaths and chiropractors. The machine uses the acupuncture points (which are in the etheric body), to get readings on each organ system of the body and to register disease at the sub-clinical level. These are proving to be very accurate devices, though as yet, most medical doctors fail to recognize them. Healing a disease pattern in the subtle body proves much easier than waiting for it to condense into physical matter, because once it does that, it becomes much more resistant to change.

Emotional Garbage

Quantum physicists have actually proven that emotions condense as energy particles, which, if not expressed as emotion, become lodged in the spaces between atoms and molecules. That literally is the filter becoming clogged. Once the emotion has become a particle, it becomes much more difficult to release, and therein lies the problem. It takes much more time and effort to release that block from the physical body than it would have if it had been released while still in pure energy form in the subtle body(s) — in this case the emotional body.

However, shifting those particles before they do harm is possible, and the best way I know to do so involves a combination of Radical Forgiveness and Satori-Breathwork. (See Part 4, Chapter 26). However, if those particles are left to accumulate and coagulate into a mass that one day becomes a cancer, the problem becomes highly intractable and, subsequently, life-threatening.

Why We Don't Heal

Clearly, time and healing are directly related. For us to evolve to the extent that we can heal ourselves, we must have most of our consciousness in present time — not in the past, not in the future, but in the *now*. Caroline Myss, in her tape series, "Why People Don't Heal," maintains that people with more than 60 percent of their life energy siphoned off to maintain the past are unable to heal themselves energetically. Thus, they remain totally reliant upon chemical medicine for their healing.

She argues that if it takes 60 to 70 percent of the average person's precious life-force to manage the negative experiences of his or her childhood, adolescence and earlier years of adulthood, as well as to hold on to the losses,

disappointments and resentments of the past, and another
10 percent worrying about, planning for and trying to control the future, that leaves precious little energy for the
present moment — or for healing. (It is important to note
that it does not drain our energy to maintain positive memories nor even negative memories if they have been pro-
cessed and forgiven.)

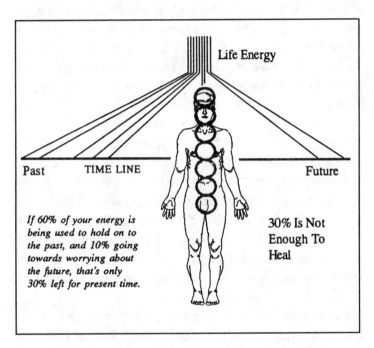

Fig. 10: Why People Don't Heal

Life has its own way of bringing us — and our energy —
into present time. Often it is through trauma. When we
find ourselves in the midst of a disaster, have an unexpected accident or discover that our lives suddenly are in

danger, we become very focused on the present moment. We bring all our consciousness into the present instinctively. Suddenly, the past does not matter. The future does not matter. Only this moment exists. The power of such currently-focused energy is demonstrated when a mother, seeing her child trapped under a car, suddenly becomes able to lift the car off the ground so her child can be rescued. Acts of incredible bravery and courage also happen when energy becomes focused in the moment, because fear only occurs when we bring the past into the future. When we are truly in the moment we are absolutely fearless, because we have no awareness of past or future.

Radical Forgiveness helps us be in present time, because we do not forgive radically by going back into the past. We simply forgive the person who happens to be mirroring our projection right here in the present. That is the beauty of Radical Forgiveness. It is true that sometimes the past connection will be so clear, as in Jill's case, it illuminates the current situation. However, the focus was still on the perfection of what was happening *in the now*.

We can either choose to let go of the victim archetype and bring our energy into the present through Radical Forgiveness or wait for a significant trauma to force us into the now. In other words, we can either transform our consciousness as a matter of will, or we can wait for a disaster or a life threatening illness to make us bring our energy into present time so we can heal our fractured souls.

13: As Above — So Below

W e, as an entire species, could soon be faced with the same choice facing each one of us as individuals. As was pointed out in the previous chapter, the choice is to heal by choice or trauma. Collectively, we must change mass consciousness or face unprecedented trauma at such a level that all the existing structures maintaining our present consciousness will be swept away to make way for the new and to let in the light.

Heal By Choice Or Trauma

Many modern visionaries claim that all the signs are present that point toward humankind receiving a massive demonstration of the *heal by choice or trauma principle* in the very near future.

Earth Changes

From earliest times right up to the present time, massive and disastrous Earth changes have been predicted for the early years of the new millenium. Predictions include two polar shifts, dramatic earthquakes, drastically-altered weather patterns, volcanic eruptions, and a significant rise in sea levels as polar ice-caps melt. The result of such events would be a radically changed map of the world with much of what we see today as land disappearing under water (most of Europe and a large chunk of western United States for example) and new continents rising from the sea. The resulting disruption and chaos would be unimaginable and millions of people would die.

Such predictions were most notably made by the famous *seer* of the 11th century, Nostra Damas, and in this century by Edgar Cayce, the *sleeping prophet,* who made very precise predictions in the 1940's. They also appear in many religious writings, including the Bible's Book of Revelations and in the traditional texts of the Mayans, the Hopi Indians and many other spiritually-aware indigenous peoples. Gordon Michael Scallion, a present-day seer, receives precise information from *spiritual sources* about the most current predictions.

It is clear to many that these *earth changes* have already begun. As the effects of global warming become impossible to ignore, the scientific community is making its own series of predictions based on the world-wide increase in floods, droughts, hurricanes, tornadoes, and volcanic eruptions, all of which bear close resemblance to the more esoteric predictions of Cayce, Scallion and others.

Consciousness Counts

The scientists do not talk much about the effects of consciousness on the earth, preferring instead to focus on what action we should take to prevent impending doom. However, the more spiritually-oriented predictions always have carried with them the caveat that the severity of the earth changes may be mitigated to the extent that we human beings come to our senses and change our consciousness. In other words, even though our fear/greed-based consciousness has wounded the etheric body of the planet so badly that a violent eruption in its physical form seems inevitable, we still can lessen the effect by raising our consciousness.

Just as we have learned that a disease pattern in the etheric body of a human being can be healed by non-physical means (prayer, Reiki, imagery, hands-on-healing, Radical Forgiveness, etc.), so the pattern of upheaval and violent change already set in the Earth's etheric body similarly can be dissipated before it manifests in the physical.

Healing Crisis

This option still remains open to us, but the window of opportunity is closing fast. Consciousness does appear to be changing to some degree, and perhaps even a partial shift will help mitigate the degree of upheaval. However, it remains difficult to imagine a worldwide shift of sufficient magnitude to heal the planet to the degree that it does not have to undergo this *healing crisis.*

(A healing crisis occurs when an organism goes through what looks like a dramatic worsening of its condition, such as with a fever or an eruption of boils, just before it starts to get well again. This worsened condition serves as a cleansing and detoxification process.)

The Earth Has Cancer

The Earth has a cancer called the human race. This living, breathing, conscious planet has been in a state of perfect balance its entire life with every little part doing what it must to sustain the system in balance. This is analogous to the job done by healthy cells in the human body. For millions of years we have been part of that balanced system. In the last few hundred years, however, we have put ourselves above the natural order and have come to believe that we can control and dominate the entire system. Just as a cancer cell multiplies out of control, metastasizes throughout the system and begins to devour its host, so we continue to multiply exponentially out of control all over the planet and to plunder its natural resources as if nothing else mattered beyond the satisfaction of our greed. Like a tumor wrapping itself around the heart or blocking a lung, so do we, in the same kind of deadly embrace with our own life-source, chop down forests, pollute the very air that we breathe and poison the environment.

All In Divine Order

No matter how drastic things get, we must believe that there is perfection and Divine purpose even in this kind of situation. After all, who could possibly have imagined a more dramatic way for Spirit to lovingly mirror our own lust for control and greed than this? We cannot evolve spiritually while holding on to these energies, and if it takes Earth changes to bring us to a healing of them, so be it. The planet will be healed in the process.

Focus On The Perfection

To put this whole discussion in perspective we must also keep in mind that, since the physical world actually is an illusion, what we experience as Earth changes will be illusionary, too. That explains why a change in human consciousness can change the situation immediately. How we experience Earth changes depends upon our perception of what is happening. If we see it as a purification of consciousness and a healing crisis that will result in a spiritual transformation, our experience of it will be in stark contrast to what we will feel if we take the victim position and think of it as real, as something to be feared and as a punishment for our rank stupidity. A Radical Forgiveness perspective will enable us to stay focused on the perfection of what is happening in the moment and will carry us through to the joy and peace on the other side of the experience.

The Gift

The adage *as above — so below* is meaningful too in terms of how we respond to the cancers in our bodies and the cancer on the planet. Waging *war* on cancer with toxic drugs and other *violent* treatment will never work; violent, high-tech, politically motivated solutions to the Earth's problems wont work either. The only thing that will work, in both cases, is *love.* When we really comprehend this, we will have understood the gift of both the Earth changes and cancer.

No lesson is more crucial than this one. People with cancer are brave souls come to the physical plane with

135

a mission to demonstrate the futility of projecting anger and war on the body and on ourselves. Their mission is make us understand that the only answer to any situation is *love*.

Visions Of Joy, Harmony and Peace

Whether or not we raise our vibration sufficiently to prevent trauma and come into loving resonance with all of life voluntarily, the end result ultimately will be the same. All the predictions about Earth changes speak of a breakthrough in consciousness happening in the wake of the Earth cleansing itself and balancing the karma we have created.

Visions of life after the Earth changes being wonderfully harmonious, peaceful and idyllic, in stark contrast to the way it is today, is a common theme running through many of the predictions. Like all healing opportunities, we can heal our soul pain at the first sign of the repressed pain occurring, or wait until it takes a disaster to wake us. However the Earth changes occur and at whatever level of destruction the planetary karma plays out, the changes will constitute the ultimate healing crisis for the planet and all of us. That will certainly be in Divine order.

To raise our vibration enough to change the predictions might include living our lives based on love and gentle acceptance of ourselves and others, forgiving ourselves for abusing the planet, joining in prayer for a planetary healing with as many people as possible from around the world involved and embracing Radical Forgiveness as nothing less than a permanent way of life.

PART THREE

Assumptions Expanded

14: Articles of Faith

The assumptions listed in Chapter Two were made briefly to give you just enough of an understanding of them to comprehend the theory of Radical Forgiveness. Now I would like to discuss in greater depth any assumptions underlying Radical Forgiveness that heretofore have not been comprehensively discussed. Hopefully, this will help you find a level of comfort with them, even if you cannot accept them totally.

Remember, all theories are based upon assumptions, but not all assumptions are proven with evidence of their validity. This holds especially true when dealing with theories and assumptions pertaining to the nature of reality and spiritual issues.

Interestingly, science and mysticism have come to a new level of agreement about the nature of reality and other spiritual questions that until now have seemed beyond the reach of science. For centuries, Hindu mystics have claimed to possess a *direct knowing* of these universal truths, which they claim to have arrived at as a result of 40 years of meditating in Himalayan caves. By using rigorous scientific methods and theoretical constructs, scientists recently have arrived at the same truths — or, should we say, have made similar assumptions. It is now safe to say that quantum physics actually demonstrates the truth of what the mystics have known for centuries. How exciting it is to see a joining of these two distinct ways of approaching and arriving at truth. Science and spirituality have come together at last with scientists becoming modern day mystics!

Yet, in spite of the progress we have made, in all humility we must continue to keep in mind that these assumptions, by their very nature, do not represent *the whole truth*. The great mystery of how the universe works and of the higher purpose of human life still seems to lie beyond mere mortal understanding, and it seems the assumptions we make are mere approximations of what might be the truth. On this basis, therefore, the following assumptions are given as the foundation for Radical Forgiveness.

Assumption: **Contrary to most Western religious thought, we are not human beings having an occasional spiritual experience. Rather we are spiritual beings having a human experience.**

This is not just a play on words. It represents a fundamental shift in our thinking about who we are and our relationship with God. Instead of thinking of ourselves as fallen and separated from God, it suggests that we are still very much connected to the All That Is and that life in a physical body is just a temporary interlude taken for the purpose of learning and balancing karma. It also suggests that God lives within each of us rather than *up there*, highlighting our dual *man/spirit* nature. Pulitzer Prize winner, Ernst Becker explained this vividly by saying, "Man is a God who shits."*

Phenomenal power exists in the idea that we are spiritual beings having a human experience. It represents a direct threat to the Ego, which consists of a cluster of beliefs that convince us we have separated from God and are subject to His wrath for committing that original sin of separation. If we, indeed, are not separate at all but totally connected, the Ego ceases to exist.

Assumption: **We have physical bodies that die, but we are immortal. In fact, our souls each may have incarnated many, many times before.**

For centuries philosophers have debated the make-up of the "soul." This discussion predates even Plato and Socrates, both of whom had much to say about the soul but remained very much at odds on the subject. Today, the debate continues with little agreement on what constitutes the soul.

Definition Of Soul

For the purposes of this discussion, however, the soul is defined as that part of us that is pure consciousness connected to the greater ocean of consciousness that forms The All That Is. Yet, for the purposes of our incarnation,

---

*Becker. E. *"The Denial of Death"* MacMillan Free Press, 1973,

141

the soul takes on an individual characteristic that can be likened to a single droplet of that same ocean or a little bit of *God Stuff.* Since we are a part of the ocean of The All That Is, we have always existed as a soul. The soul has no beginning and no end, exits outside of both time and space and is immortal. During our incarnation, the soul keeps us connected to the World of Divine Truth and the All That Is and is responsible for our spiritual evolution.

Once the soul incarnates, it becomes attached to both a body and a personality, which together represent a *persona* or identity. This we create for ourselves based on our own self-concept, which we present to the world at large. Thus, our soul becomes subject to the stresses of human existence and can even become sick. A great many of the sicknesses of today, such as cancer, begin as a deep sickness of the soul. Shamans speak of the soul becoming fractured and splintered, parts of it actually being left behind and lost in past events, especially traumas. A great deal of a shaman's healing work revolves around the idea of soul retrieval.

Reincarnation has been an issue of contention through the ages as well, and many churches and religions will not consider this idea even today. Yet, Eastern religions have always included reincarnation among their spiritual beliefs. Past life regression, mediumship, psychic phenomena all seem to support this assumption.

The best evidence we have of death being a transition into an afterlife comes from the vast pool of people who have had near-death experiences. These accounts are so similar in their content and quality they hardly can be refuted. Thousands of people have reported similar kinds of experiences and exhibit the same kind of certainty that what they saw was real. The effect near death experiences have on their lives are more or less identical as well.

It appears that not only do our souls incarnate numerous times but that they do not come into this physical life experience alone. Based on the past life research, it seems likely that our souls keep coming back time and time again with others from our soul group to resolve particular *karmic* imbalances. During our journey towards wholeness, we create energy imbalances that have to be restored. These imbalances are referred to as our karma. For example, if we take advantage of people and cheat them, we must at some time have the experience of being cheated to equalize the energy. This is not a moral exercise; it has nothing to do with right or wrong. As we have already noted, the Universe is neutral. This happens simply as a balancing of energy and is dictated by the Law of Cause and Effect, which states that for every action there must be an equal reaction. (See Chapter 8.)

The people with whom we play and the games we play with them are all about balancing energy in this manner. Our soul heals and becomes whole again each time we rebalance the karmic energies. Thus, each incarnation contributes to the healing of the soul.

Incidentally, since time does not exist in the world of Divine Truth, all our incarnations happen simultaneously. As we heal in one lifetime, we heal all the other incarnations as well. Use of Radical Forgiveness in one lifetime, therefore, provides incredible value to a soul, because it heals all the other incarnations at the same time as it heals the current one. Imagine the collective karma that was balanced by Nelson Mandela forgiving a whole generation of whites in South Africa for their treatment of blacks. By the same token, imagine the collective karma that remains to be balanced in America for the treatment of slaves and the Native American Indians.

Our Soul always moves us in the direction of healing and keeps creating situations that offer us the opportunity to balance karmic energy. However, if this healing is not accomplished at the level of Divine Truth, we tend to recreate the imbalance through the resentment and revenge cycle and the maintenance of victim consciousness. This keeps the wheel of karma spinning round and round and round. Radical Forgiveness provides one of the best ways to stop the wheel from turning, because it breaks the cycle.

Assumption: **While our bodies and our senses tell us we are separate individuals, in truth we are all one. We all individually vibrate as part of a single whole.**

We are not our bodies. We are not our Egos. We are not our personality selves or the roles we play each day. Believing we are these things serves as a clever device used by the Ego to disguise our true essence from ourselves and from others and to keep us locked into the belief that we

144

are just our bodies and our personalities. Upholding this belief makes it impossible for us to remember who we really are — an individual soul created as part of God and existing in oneness with God.

Assumption: **When all our souls were one with God, we experimented with a thought that separation was possible. We became trapped in that thought, which became the illusion or dream that we now live. It is a dream because, contrary to the idea of original sin, the separation did not actually happen. We only think it did — and that thought gave birth to the Ego.**

Once we were completely enfolded in the All That Is — God. We were formless, unchanging, immortal, and knew only love. Then, we had a thought. What would it be like, we wondered, if we were to descend into physical reality and experience the opposite energies — such as form, change, separation, fear, death, limitation, and duality? We played with the idea for a while, always thinking we could withdraw from the experiment any time we wished, should we indeed decide to put the thought into action. We saw no danger. Thus, the decision was made, and we lowered our energetic vibration to condense our energy into physical form. In the process, we forgot our connection to God and imagined we had actually separated from God and that we had no way back to The All That Is.

This dream became very real for us, and we grew extremely guilt ridden for committing this *(original)* sin of

145

separating from God. We became fearful that God would bring his wrath down upon us for having done so. This powerful belief in sin, guilt and fear became the Ego, and it became such a powerful force in our lives that it created in our minds a world dominated by fear. Our world is still one where fear, rather than love, is the driving force.

Though we tend to personify it, the Ego is not an entity in and of itself. Neither does it represent our personality. The Ego represents a set of deeply-held beliefs that keep us totally convinced of our separateness from God. The extreme power exerted by these subconscious beliefs through the dynamics of guilt, fear, repression, and projection create the appearance that the Ego *lives* in us. The Ego keeps us stuck in the World of Humanity and asleep (unconscious) dreaming that we have separated from God.

Assumption: **When we decided to experiment with physical incarnation, God gave us total free will to live this experiment in any way we chose and to find for ourselves the way home to the All That Is.**

Free will is honored at the highest level. Contrary to what the Ego would have us believe, God was not mad at us for playing with the idea of separation. God gives us anything we want, whatever we choose and makes no judgment about it. However, when we ask for help, through prayer and Radical Forgiveness, the call is always answered.

Assumption: **Life is not a random event. It has purpose and provides the unfoldment of a divine plan with opportunities to make choices and decisions in every moment.**

Seen from the World of Humanity, it might appear that we arrive on this planet by biological accident. Our only significance lies in the fact that our parents made love and started a chain of biological events called pregnancy and birth.

It also might appear as if the only way to master the life experience lies in learning a lot about how the world works and in developing skills that enable us to control as much as possible the seemingly random circumstances of our lives. The more mastery we achieve over the physical circumstances of our lives, the better our lives appear to become.

The opposite is true when viewed from the World of Divine Truth. From this perspective, our arrival on the planet represents a deliberate, planned and conscious choice. The plan includes the selection of the people who will serve as our parents. Also, the seemingly haphazard events of our lives are attributed to the unfoldment of a divine plan, decided upon in advance, and totally purposeful in terms of our spiritual growth. The more we surrender to this unfoldment without trying to control it, the happier we become.

At first blush, this seems a fatalistic viewpoint. However,

147

this is not just fate. In truth, the divine plan allows for a great deal of creativity and flexibility and continues to honor the principle of free will. We continue to co-create with Spirit the circumstances of our lives and, without exception, to get precisely what we want. The extent to which we resist (judge) what we get, determines whether we experience life as painful or joyful.

Mastery of the life experience, then, relies on us entering life fully and trusting that we are taken care of totally and supported all the time no matter what. Radical Forgiveness moves us in that direction.

Assumption: **Physical reality is an illusion created by our five senses. Matter consists of interrelating energy fields vibrating at different frequencies.**

Most people have a difficult time coming to grips with the idea that our physical reality is an illusion created by our senses. Ken Carey confirms the difficulty we have grasping this concept. In his book, which was a channeled work, the souls *talking through him* made an interesting observation.* They said that when they got inside Carey's body and experienced all his senses, they were simply amazed. Only then did they understand why human beings felt the physical world was real. Our senses make the illusion so convincing that even these disincarnate souls appreciated why we would have great difficulty getting beyond it.

---

* Carey. K. "Starseed Transmissions" (Uni*Sun, 1982),

Indeed, it is difficult to remember that the physical world is simply an illusion. However, we are beginning to move in a direction that fosters that memory. Recently, scientists have begun talking about the human body in terms of a *mind/body continuum.* Such terminology gives us the sense that our bodies are, indeed, more than cells, molecules and atoms. Energy science tells us that, in reality, our bodies are *dense condensations of interrelating energy fields* and that, just like a hologram, all matter consists of energy vibrating in certain patterns. Holograms are those seemingly real, three-dimensional images created by laser beams. Quantum physicists have theorized that the entire universe is a hologram and everything in it, including each one of us, is a hologram as well.

Some energy fields vibrate at frequencies that enable them to be observed and measured. They can be given physical qualities like weight, volume, hardness, and fluidity. We give such energy patterns names like wood, steel, leather, or whisky. Everything physical simply represents energy vibrating at a rate we can *detect* with our five senses.

Yet, this concept seems strange to us. We have developed such faith in our five senses to detect the physical world around us that we have difficulty imagining that our bodies consist of more than just what we can see and feel. Yet, in a very real sense, the physical world is an illusion *created* by our senses.

Consider for a moment one of the metal beams holding up a building. It looks solid enough, and our sense of touch

149

and sight tell us that it is solid, as well as strong and heavy. However, we also know that this beam is composed entirely of atoms. Our knowledge of atoms tells us that each atom is composed of a nucleus of protons around which orbits at ultra high speed one or more electrons.

To get a feel for the relationship between the nucleus and the electron, think of a basketball sitting in the middle of a football stadium. Now imagine an object the size of a golf ball orbiting the basketball and taking up the entire volume of the stadium as it swings around at several thousand miles per hour. That picture roughly is equivalent to the ratio between the size of the electron and the nucleus and the space between the two.

We can say that an atom is composed of somewhere around 99.99% space. Since matter is composed entirely of atoms, matter must be composed of 99.99% space. Thus, the aforementioned beam is 99.99% space. *You* are 99.99% space as well.

The beam looks so dense for the same reason that an electric fan when running looks solid. When such a fan is not rotating you can see the spaces between the blades, and you can put your hand through those spaces. When the blades spin very fast, you can no longer see the spaces. In addition, if you try putting your hand between the blades, they feel like an impenetrable wall. Like a fan's blades, any piece of physical material is comprised of a mass of electrons spinning so fast that they appear solid to our senses.

150

If the electrons in the beam holding up the building were to stop spinning, the beam would disappear in an instant. If all the other electrons around it stopped spinning too, we could imagine the whole building disappearing. No debris would be left, no dust, nothing. To a viewer, it would appear that the building had simply evaporated or disappeared.

Matter is simply vibration — nothing more, nothing less. Our senses are tuned to these vibrations, and our minds convert them into matter. Sounds weird, but it's true.

Assumption: **We have subtle bodies as well as physical bodies. Our physical body vibrates at the frequency of matter (the World of Humanity), while the highest two of the five subtle bodies vibrate closer to the frequency of the Soul (the World of Divine Truth).**

Besides the flesh and bone of our physical bodies, we consist of other energy patterns we cannot see or measure. These are called our *subtle bodies* or *subtle fields*. They vibrate at frequencies an octave or two higher than those bodies condensed as matter and are beyond the range of our senses and most detection instrumentation. These are:

The Etheric Body
The etheric body carries the energetic template of the body. It ensures the continuation of the patterns, harmonies and disharmonies within the body while the body constantly renews itself. Your body is not the same one as one year

151

ago, for not one cell exists in your body that is more than one year old.

The etheric body interacts with your genetic code and holds the memory of who you are, the shape of your nose, your height, what prejudices you hold, what you like to eat, your strengths, your weakness, your illness patterns, etc.

The Emotional Body
The emotional body vibrates one octave above the etheric field. Also known as the astral body, it suffuses the etheric field and the bioenergetic fields of the physical body and manifests in the body as feelings.

An emotion constitutes a thought attached to a feeling that usually results in a physical response or action. When energy flows freely from the emotional field through the etheric field and the physical body, everything works together beautifully.

When we restrict our emotional energy through suppression or repression, we create energy blocks in both our etheric and emotional fields as well as in our physical body.

The perceptual shift required for forgiveness cannot happen while anger and resentment are maintained in the emotional body. Any energy stuck in the emotional body must be cleared first.

The Mental Body
This field governs our intellectual functioning and is

responsible for memory, rational thinking, concrete thought, and so on. Of course, there are scientists who still maintain that thinking and other mental processing can be explained in terms of brain biochemistry. Suffice it to say that the scientists who follow the logic of quantum physics believe that the mind goes beyond the brain, beyond even the body. They believe that brain and mind interact *holographically* and that each cell contains a blueprint of the whole. Many researchers believe that memory resides in holographic form in an energetic field that exists beyond the body.

Proof of this is continually showing up as a by-product of organ replacement surgery. One celebrated story concerns a person who received a liver transplant. Some months after the operation, he began having a recurring dream that did not make sense to him. After some investigation, he discovered that the person who had donated the liver had dreamt the same dream for many years. The memory of that dream was apparently imbedded in the cellular structure of the liver.

The Causal Body or Intuitional Field
At the next octave up lies the body we might call our soul, Higher Self or our connection to the World of Divine Truth. Also called the causal body, this one provides our bridge to the spiritual realm. Whereas the mental field deals with ideas and thought forms at the concrete level, this field deals with them at the conceptual, abstract, iconic, and symbolic level. It deals with essence, intuition and *direct knowing*. The causal body extends beyond the individual

and penetrates the *collective mind* — or what Jung called the *collective unconscious,* a single mind to which we all individually connect and which all we can access.

The idea of subtle bodies rising in harmonics is by no means new; it has been included in many great spiritual traditions throughout the whole world, especially those of the East.

Assumption: **Universal energy as life force and consciousness is brought into our body via the chakra system. The first three chakras are aligned with the World of Humanity while the fourth through eighth align more closely with the World of Divine Truth.**

In addition to the ocean of energy containing our differently-vibrating subtle bodies, we human beings posses a system of energy centers that align vertically in our bodies. These are known as chakras — *wheels of energy* in Sanskrit, because they are like vortices of spinning energy.

The chakras act like transformers. They take the energy or life force (prana, chi, Christ energy) that comes to us from the universe and step it down to frequencies that can be used by the bio-molecular and cellular processes of the physical body. The chakras also represent the locations where each of the subtle bodies link to the physical body, thus bringing different levels of consciousness into our being. They process our daily experiences, thoughts and feelings while also carrying long-term data relating to personal and tribal history, long-established thought patterns and archetypes.

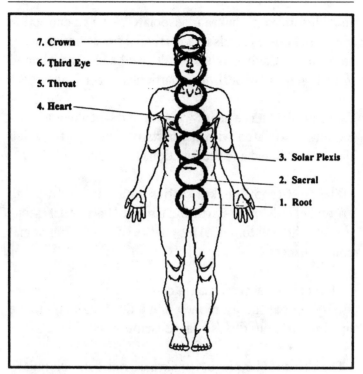

Fig 11: The Human Chakra System.

The first three chakras possess levels of consciousness vibrating at the lower frequencies of the existential chain and rooted in the World of Humanity. They carry the energy of the victim archetype. Mock Forgiveness is the only type of forgiveness possible with the consciousness of the first three chakras. The consciousness that comes through the fifth, six, seventh, and eighth chakras are more likely to align with energies from the World of Divine Truth, while the fourth, the heart chakra, provides the link between the World of Humanity and the World of Divine Truth.

In addition, each chakra is associated with an endocrine gland and corresponds to a particular nerve nexus in the same area. Each also has a color and sound associated with it, and each nourishes a particular part of the body.

Chakras also serve as information data-banks and processors associated with the parts of the body to which they are attached and the functions they serve.

• The **first** (root) chakra carries data relating to being grounded to Mother Earth and issues of basic trust, security and the will to live. This chakra runs on tribal/social consciousness.

• The **second** (sacral) chakra carries data relating to creativity, sexual energy, money, and guilt. This chakra, like the first, runs on tribal/social consciousness.

• The **third** (solar plexus) chakra carries data relating to power and control, social and familial relationships, betrayal, and anger. This chakra also is directed by tribal/social consciousness.

• The **fourth** (heart) chakra carries data about matters of the heart, relationships, love, nurturing, and compassion. This is the first chakra to energize individuality and self-determination independent of social group consciousness.

• The **fifth** chakra (throat) carries data about things expressed or withheld in matters of personal power, individual will and creative expression. It is directed by individual, as opposed to group, consciousness.

• The **sixth** (3rd eye) chakra carries data relative to intuitive knowledge, clairvoyance and the will to know the truth. In this case, truth refers to knowing not defined by group consciousness, but directly from individual experience.

• The **seventh** (crown) chakra carries data about spiritual awareness and connection to Source.

• The **eighth** chakra, which lies above the head, represents our contract or agreement for incarnation and contains our life's mission.

Though central to eastern medical traditions, the chakra system gets zero attention from western medical science and there exists very little recognition generally in the west of its central importance to our health, spiritual wellbeing and vibratory rate.

In truth, they are crucial. When these energy centers become out of balance — as they do when we become emotionally upset or traumatized for instance — they reverse rotation, become very erratic and in some cases close down almost entirely. Anger, resentment and hurt will tend to close the heart chakra and the throat chakra, guilt and lack of trust will weaken the sacral chakra, and so on. The effects of such energy imbalances will be felt as lethargy, a general malaise, low sex drive, inability to speak our truth and a whole host of symptoms for which a medical cause cannot be found. If the chakras remain out of balance for a long time however, it is inevitable that an effect will indeed, sooner or later, manifest as disease in the physical body. As we noted with the subtle bodies, disease almost always begins in the energy fields — which include the chakras — and moves into the physical body appearing finally as disease or physical breakdown.

Fortunately, chakras can be restored to balance quite easily. There are practitioners who are sensitive enough to feel the energy of each chakra and have techniques for rebalancing them. Most forms of energy medicine such as acupuncture, homeopathy, aromatherapy and many others act directly on the chakras and bring them into balance.

(For a thorough explanation of how our evolution can be explained by reference to the chakras, see "Anatomy of the Spirit," by Caroline Myss, (Three Rivers Press, 1996.)

PART FOUR

Tools For Radical Forgiveness

15: Fake It 'Til You Make It

All forgiveness begins as false forgiveness. No forgiveness tool exists that enables us to forgive instantly. Even the tools provided in this section do not make us forgive, they ask us simply to express our *willingness* to forgive. Using them represents an act of faith, a prayer, an offering, a humble request for Divine assistance. They help us make forward movement.

In the Seattle study on forgiveness mentioned in Chapter 12, the participants were *faking* forgiveness simply by taking part in the experiment. Their very participation served as an expression of their willingness to forgive. Only later did they actually *make it,* and even then they achieved forgiveness through no any effort of their own.

Surrendering

Faking it until you make it really means surrendering to the process, putting forth no efforting nor trying to control the results. In the study, the more effort the participants put into trying to forgive, the more difficult they found it to let go of their hurt and anger. When they stopped trying to forgive and to control the process, at some point in time forgiveness just happened.

It is true that the energetic shift from anger and blame to forgiveness and responsibility happens much more quickly with Radical Forgiveness, because, using the tools given here, we can drop the victim consciousness. Consciousness, you will recall, changes time.

Nevertheless, even with Radical Forgiveness we must enter the process with no expectation of when an energy shift might happen. Each time we forgive radically, we surely move energy. However, if we have a great deal of residual pain around an issue, it might take months or even years to feel unconditional love for the person involved.

Only when we feel unconditional love for the person do we know we have finished the process of forgiveness. Feeling neutral does not mean the process is complete. We need not like the person or love the person's personality, but we must feel love for the person's soul to experience Radical Forgiveness. When we feel this unconditional love for their soul, our soul joins theirs and we become one.

Seeing The Opportunity

Any time someone upsets us, we must recognize this emotion as an opportunity to forgive. The person upsetting us may be resonating something in us that we need to heal, in which case, he or she gives us a gift, if we care to see it that way — if we care to *shift our perception*. The situation also may be a replay of earlier times when someone did something similar to us. If so, this current person represents all the people who have ever done this to us before. As we forgive this person for the current situation, we forgive all others who behaved likewise, as well as forgiving ourselves for what we might have projected onto them.

Shifting Our Perception

The following chapters contain processes that shift energy and offer opportunities to *change our perception* of what might be happening in a given situation. This change in perception constitutes the essence of Radical Forgiveness. All of these processes bring us into the present moment by helping us retrieve our energy from the past and withdraw it from the future, both of which must be done for change to occur. When we are in the present moment, we cannot feel resentment, because resentment only lives in the past. Neither can we feel fear, because fear only exists in relation to the future. We find ourselves, therefore, with the opportunity to be in present time and in the space of love, acceptance and Radical Forgiveness.

First Aid Forgiveness Tools

Some of the tools included in this section are more appropriate for use at the very moment when a situation requiring forgiveness occurs. They help jerk us into an awareness of what may be happening before we get drawn too deeply into a drama. When our *buttons get pushed,* we easily move straight into the defense/attack cycle. Once in this cycle, however, we find it tough to get out. The Ego has the upper hand, and we basically fall into unconsciousness. Use of these quick tools, however, helps us avoid ever beginning the cycle.

163

Others tools described in the following chapters are designed for use in quiet solitude after we have had a chance to vent anger and frustration. Of all the tools, I believe that the Radical Forgiveness Worksheet is the most profound for it has the ability to take us all the way home. (See Chapter 29.)

Use them all as an act of faith in the beginning. The payoff will prove incredible in time. Consistent use of these tools helps us find a peace we may never have known was even possible. Plus, our relationships will improve, we will become healthier and we will feel so abundant we will hardly be able to stand it!

16: Feeling The Pain

The forgiveness process requires that we give ourselves permission to feel the feelings we have around a given situation — and to feel them fully. If we try to forgive using a purely mental process, thus denying that we feel angry, sad, or depressed, for example, nothing happens. It simply becomes mental masturbation masquerading as forgiveness.

It also needs to be understood that there is no such thing as a negative emotion. They only become *bad* and have a negative effect on us when they are suppressed, denied or unexpressed.

We Want The Emotional Experience

As human beings, we are blessed with the capability to feel emotions. In fact, some say the *only* reason we have chosen this human experience arises from the fact that this is the only planet carrying the vibration of emotional energy, and we have come here precisely to experience it. Consequently, when we do not allow ourselves to experience emotions and suppress them instead, our souls create situations in which we literally are forced to feel them.

This means that the whole point of creating an upset may simply lie in our soul's desire to provide an opportunity for us to feel a suppressed emotion. If that is the case, simply allowing ourselves to have the feeling, free from the thoughts we have about it, might allow the energy to move through us and the so-called problem to disappear.

However, not all situations are dissolved that easily. When we try coping with a deep-seated issue and a remembrance of what seems an unforgivable transgression, such as sexual abuse, rape or physical abuse, it takes more than just experiencing our emotions to get to the point where we feel unconditional love for that person.

Feeling The Emotion Comes First

In most cases, feeling the emotion fully is just the first step in faking it until we make it and definitely cannot be bypassed. I am not saying that the emotional work will not benefit from insight gained through a shift in perception that might normally come a step later in the forgiveness process. It certainly will. However, the converse does not hold true; the perceptual shift required for Radical Forgiveness will not happen if the underlying repressed feelings are not released first.

Invariably, when we feel the desire to forgive someone or something, we have at some time felt anger toward them or it. Anger actually exists as a secondary emotion. Beneath anger lies a primary emotional pain, such as hurt pride, shame, frustration, sadness, terror, or fear. Anger represents *energy in motion* emanating from the suppression of that pain. Not allowing one's anger to flow can be likened to trying to cap a volcano. One day it surely will blow!

Stage one in the Radical Forgiveness process asks us to get in touch with not only the anger, but the underlying emotion as well. This means feeling it — not talking about it, not analyzing it, not labeling it, but experiencing it!

Love Your Anger

All too often when people talk about *letting go* of anger or *releasing* anger, they really mean trying to get rid of it. They judge it as wrong and undesirable — even frightening. They do not want to feel it so they talk about it and try to process it intellectually, but that does not work.

Trying to release emotion represents resistance to feeling it, and there is truth in the saying **what you resist persists**. Since anger represents energy in motion, resisting it just keeps it stuck within us — until the volcano erupts. Releasing anger actually means freeing the stuck energy of held emotions by allowing them to move freely through the body as feeling. Doing some kind of *anger work* helps us experience this emotion purposely and with control.

Anger Work

This can be as simple as screaming into a cushion (so as not to alarm neighbors), yelling in the car, beating cushions, chopping wood, or doing some other explosive

167

physical activity. Combining physical activity with the use of the voice seems to provide the key to successful anger work. All too often we block the energy of anger in the throat, so vocal expression should always be a part of the process. We should go into it, not with the idea of trying to rid ourselves of the anger, but with the intention of feeling the intensity of it moving through our body — without thought or judgment. If we truly can surrender to the emotions, we will feel more alive than we have felt in a long while, and we will find that the anger has dissipated.

If Anger Is Scary

For many of us, the thought of bringing up anger may be too scary even to contemplate, especially if terror lies underneath the anger. The person who did these terrible things to us may still exert a strong influence on our subconscious mind. Under these circumstances, it would not be advisable to do anger work alone. Instead, we should work with someone who knows how to support us while we feel both the anger and the terror — someone with whom we feel safe and who has experience in helping people move through intense emotion. A counselor or psychotherapist of some kind would be a good choice.

I also recommend doing Satori Breathwork (See Chapter 26), with a skilled practitioner. This provides a wonderful way to release emotion and can be done in a group or one-on-one.

Anger Addiction Warning

A note of caution needs to be sounded here. It becomes all too easy to get addicted to anger. Anger feeds on itself and easily becomes resentment. Resentment relishes going over and over an old hurt, constantly revisiting the pain associated with it and venting the resultant anger in some form. It becomes a powerful addiction in and of itself.

We must realize that, except inasmuch as it makes us feel good for a short while, anger that persists serves no useful purpose. Consequently, once the energy of anger has been allowed to flow as feeling, we should use the energy to create a positive outcome. Maybe we need to set a boundary or a condition on future interactions with the person around whom our anger revolves. Perhaps we can make a decision of some kind, such as to be willing to feel compassion for the person or to forgive the person. Only when used as the catalyst for positive change, self-empowerment or forgiveness will we prevent the anger from becoming an addictive cycle.

17: The Forgiveness List

W hen beginning the forgiveness process, it can prove helpful to make a list of all the people against whom we hold grudges or hold judgments or whom we blame for something that happened to us — in short, a list of anyone we need to forgive.

To do this, list the name of such people on a piece of paper along with a brief reminder of what you resent about them. Then, using a scale of 1 to 100, give each person a number representing how much negative energy you might be holding about them or the situation you feel they caused. (Do *not* include yourself on the list.)

Do not dwell on this list. Just keep it somewhere for reference. As you use the tools in this section of the book to do your forgiveness work, look at your list from time to time to see if any of the negative energy ratings have gone up or down. If they have decreased, look to see who or what you have been forgiving in the present that might account for the decline in negative energy around the person or situation on your list. You probably will find a correlation, for, as mentioned previously, when you forgive someone in the present you forgive everyone who ever did something similar to you in the past. Your forgiveness list provides a good feedback device in this regard. Wouldn't it be nice to bring all those ratings down to zero! It is possible.

RADICAL FORGIVENESS LIST _(Who in my life have I not yet forgiven?)_		
Name:	My Resentment Is Over.....	%

18: Spinning The Story

When something happens to us, we interpret that experience and give personal meaning to the situation. Then, we merge what really happened with our interpretation of what happened. The story we *make up* based on that mixture of fact and fiction becomes our truth and an operating principle in our lives. This insight was given to me by a graduate of a well-known seminar called The Landmark Forum, which is where he had learned it.

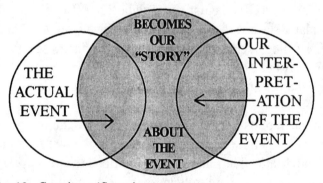

Fig. 12: Creating a 'Story.'

Example: Glenda was a sophisticated, intelligent, attractive and accomplished woman in her late 40s. She had never been married. In fact, she had never had a relationship that lasted more than two or three years. It seemed

173

she could never meet *Mr. Right.* Whenever she got to know a man well, she discovered something about him that annoyed her or made her feel dissatisfied with the relationship. So, she would end the relationship. This happened over and over again. She did not see it as a problem, though. As a career woman, she said her job provided her with a lot of satisfaction. On the other hand, she did concede that she was lonely.

One day a good friend asked her, "Have you ever wondered why you don't hold onto a relationship? Have you ever thought that maybe it's not the *something* that you see in them that makes you annoyed or dissatisfied but the *something* in you that you haven't dealt with that won't let you have a decent relationship with a man?"

At the time Glenda just shrugged off her friend's words, but later she began thinking more deeply about her friend's query. She decided to work with a therapist to see if anything lay behind her relationship pattern. The therapist hypnotized her and then regressed her to the age of eight.

Under hypnosis, she recalled that at that age every day she would come home from school to play with her best friend, Mark. They had been close friends since they were very young and were truly inseparable at this point in time. Then she recalled an incident that happened one day after she had changed out of her school clothes and run over to Mark's house. She knocked on the door, and no one answered. She put her face close to the glass and peered in. Her heart sank when she saw the house was empty. Where was everyone? Where was the furniture? Where was Mark? She did not understand — not until she turned to leave the front porch and saw a small sign lying flat in the grass. It said, 'SOLD.'

It slowly dawned on Glenda that Mark's parents had sold the house and gone away taking Mark with them — gone without saying a word, without so much as a goodbye, without even telling her. Mark had never even mentioned that he was moving.

Hurt and confused, Glenda sat on the porch for a few hours before walking the short distance home. She remembered making two decisions during that time. The first was to say nothing to her parents. If they mentioned Mark being gone, she would pretend she did not care. The second decision was never to trust a boy (man) again.

She had apparently forgotten all about this incident, but when it surfaced during her therapy session she became upset. The years of repressed grief over being abandoned by her best friend poured out as did the rage over what she saw as a betrayal.

After the session, she went to see her mother. She talked about Mark and asked her Mother what happened to him and his family. "Oh, his father got transferred," her mother said. "It all happened quite quickly, but we were very surprised that you said nothing about their leaving. We thought you'd be really upset, but you seemed to just take it in your stride. In fact we and Mark's parents talked before

175

they left, because all of us were concerned that you and Mark would be terribly upset. We all agreed it would be best in the long run if we didn't tell either of you anything about the move until the day it actually happened. They didn't even put a For Sale sign up on the house. It was not until Mark was in the car and on the way to their new home that they even told him."

Glenda was stunned. If Mark did not know about the move, then he had not betrayed her after all. At that moment the realization hit her — for more than 30 years she had allowed a completely buried subconscious idea to rule her life and to spoil every romantic relationship she had ever had. Not only that, the idea itself was based on a totally false assumption.

As soon as any man got close enough to Glenda to be her friend and her lover, she ended the relationship. She believed that if she got close to a man, like she had been with Mark, he would abandon and betray her in the same way. She was not going to risk suffering that degree of pain again, not for any man. Not only that, she shut down, or suppressed, her feelings of abandonment and betrayal on the day she discovered Mark had moved. Later, she poured herself into her career as a way of avoiding those feelings.

The friend who confronted Glenda with her self-defeating pattern saw beyond her *story* and recognized that something else was going on. She had created many healing opportunties but had missed them all. His intervention prevented her from needing to be severely abandoned again to heal the original pain.

My sister Jill did something similar. When our father demonstrated the kind of love for my daughter, Lorraine, that Jill always wanted to feel from him and had not felt, Jill took that to mean that she was inherently unlovable. That became the story she believed until she brought someone into her life who was able to aquaint her with its inaccuracy.

The Forgiveness Centrifuge

Using this tool might have saved both Jill and Glenda many years of painful struggle. The Forgiveness Centrifuge helps us separate *what actually happened* in any given situation from our *interpretation* of what happened. If you own the type of juicer where you put carrots and other things in the top and the juice is separated from the fiber by the centrifugal force of the spinning grater, you know what is meant by the term centrifuge. A centrifuge also is used to separate blood from plasma, cream from milk, and so on. A washing machine spinning out the excess water from clothes works in the same manner as well.

A forgiveness centrifuge simply reverses the process by which we come up with stories about what happened to us. To use it, take the story you are living now — the one that is causing you discomfort. Remember, it is certain to be a hopeless mixture of fact (what happened) and interpretation (all your thoughts, judgments, assessments, assumptions, and beliefs about what happened). Feed the story into the top of the imaginary centrifuge, just like you would with carrots in a juicer, and then, in your mind, see the machine separating the facts from the interpretations.

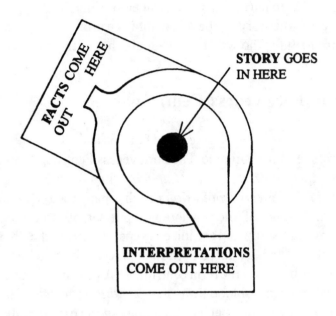

Fig. 13: Separating Fact From Fiction

Then, like any good researcher, first make a list of the facts as they emerge, being as objective as possible. Then make a list of the interpretations you made about the facts.

#	The Facts About What Happened

#	My Interpretations About What Happened

After writing down your results, acknowledge the facts and accept them. Recognize that the facts equate to what happened and that no one can do anything to change that. You have no choice but to allow what happened to be exactly that — what happened, but watch for any tendency to make excuses for what happened. If you allow this to happen, you impose interpretation on the facts once again. Just stay with what actually happened. Stay with the facts.

Next, examine every thought, belief, rationalization, idea, or attitude you imposed on what happened, and declare them all to be *untrue*. Affirm that none of them have validity. Tell yourself they just represent mind-talk.

Then, recognize how important your ideas, beliefs and attitudes are to you. Look at your *attachment* to each of them, and decide which of them you possibly are ready to drop and which you are not.

	Interpretations	Attachment

Be Gentle With Yourself

Do not criticize yourself for being attached to any of them or for being unwilling to let them go. You may have had these ideas, beliefs and attitudes for a long time. In fact, they may define who you are. For example, if you are an incest survivor or an adult child of an alcoholic, these labels, which represent ideas or beliefs about yourself, may provide a reference for who you are. If you let go of the ideas associated with these labels, you might lose your identity. So, while you want to be firm with yourself in separating what is real from what you have made up, be gentle with yourself and allow time to release these beliefs.

Please be aware that this process does not constitute Radical Forgiveness. It just helps you get clarity about your situation, and, in so doing, represents a preparatory step to Radical Forgiveness. On the other hand, just looking at the facts of the problem and comparing them to your interpretation of the problem may resolve the problem itself.

In all likelihood, though, you will need to do more forgiveness work. For instance, you may well have some self-forgiveness to do. Imagine the guilt, the anger, the depression, and the criticism you might feel and direct at yourself when you find out you have created your entire life around a set of untrue beliefs. Please, *do not* create this scenario. Instead, remember that everything has a purpose, and God does not make mistakes. Use one or more of the forgiveness tools to work on forgiving yourself and on seeing the perfection in your situation.

181

You may also need to complete a Radical Forgiveness worksheet. (See Chapter 29.) If the facts still prove that something *bad* took place — for example, a murder remains a murder no matter what interpretations you may have made, the Radical Forgiveness Worksheet provides the only tool that helps you shift the energy around the event. The rituals and other tools will help to some degree, but if you still feel victimized by what happened or you still see it as a *bad* event, the Radical Forgiveness Worksheet will help shift your energy.

Do not forget that even the facts of what happened represent an illusion. While what happens in the world happens to be *true*, these things do not represent *truth*, because they remain a projection of our consciousness.

19: Four Steps To Forgiveness

This adaptation of a three-step process taught by Arnold Patent, serves as a reminder of our power to attract the events and people we need to feel the emotions we have around a particular issue. Patent used this tool as a way to make us conscious of the fact that whatever appears to occur outside ourselves and around us results from our power to create our reality through our thoughts and beliefs.*

This process should be used during the occurrence of an upset or shortly thereafter. When you find yourself making judgments, feeling self-righteous or wanting to change something about a situation, use this process to bring your consciousness into the present, to let go of the illusion and to align with spiritual truth.

Step One: *"Look what I created."*

This first step reminds us that we are the creators of our reality. Do not assume *guilt* for what happens. Take responsibility, but do so free of any self-judgment or criticism. Being quick to judge, we often use this step as a

---

* Patent A. M. *"You Can Have It All"* Simon & Schuster, 1995 and *"Death Taxes And Other Illusions"* (Celebration Publishing, 1989).

way to *beat ourselves up.* We say, "Look what I have created. Oh, it's terrible — I must be a terrible person, a spiritual failure." Please do not fall into this trap, for, if you do, you buy into the illusion.

Step Two: *"I notice my judgments and love myself for having them."*

This step acknowledges that as humans we automatically attach a whole string of judgments, interpretations, questions, and beliefs to situations. Our task involves accepting the imperfection of our own humanity and loving ourselves for having these judgments, including the one that says we must be a bad, spiritually-moribund person for creating this reality. Our judgments are part of ourselves, so we must love them as we love ourselves. This connects us with what actually is happening in our body and mind and brings us into the present through our feelings. Our energy then shifts quickly and allows us to go to the third and fourth steps of this process.

Step Three: *"I am willing to see the perfection in the situation."*

The *willingness* step represents the essential one in any genuine forgiveness process, be it Mock or Radical. It equates to a prayerful surrendering in the moment to the Divine plan and the willingness to love ourselves for not being able to see this plan directly.

Step Four: *"I choose the power of peace."*

This fourth step represents a consequence of all the previous steps. By accepting that Divine purpose is served in this situation and that what appears to be occurring may be illusionary, we choose to feel peace and to use the power of peace in whatever actions are required of us. The power of peace is found when we are totally present in the moment, acting with clarity and focus to do whatever may be required and totally aware of our feelings.

Practice this four-step process as often as possible. Make it a part of your awareness. It gives you a way to be in the moment throughout your day.

20: The Forgiveness Rose

This meditation was taught to me by Jim Self of the Avalon Institute in Chico, California. I have adapted it to suit the Radical Forgiveness process.

When we open our hearts to others, we become vulnerable and face the danger of becoming the target for their projections. Their psychic energy can become mixed with ours, and this can deplete our energy.

The rose is a symbol of psychic protection in a great many esoteric writings. For whatever reason, it possesses a great deal of potency in this regard. Using a rose in a meditation as a protection from the projections of others offers a way to block that negative energy without closing our heart to the person. I cannot explain why the rose visualization works so well in this regard; in truth, we can create psychic protection with any kind of visualization, because just doing so creates the intention of self protection. The intention, acting as a cause, achieves the effect of actual protection. However, the rose has been used for centuries for this purpose and seems to work better than most other symbols.

The next time you encounter someone whose energy you

don't want mixed with your own, visualize the rose existing at the edge of your aura, or half-way between yourself and the person. Then notice if you feel differently while in their presence. You should feel a much greater sense of your own psychic space and identity while at the same time being totally present for the person.

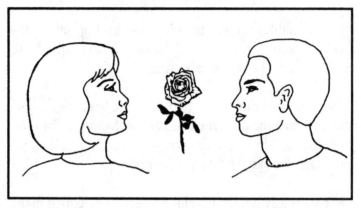

Fig. 14: The Rose.

To feel the power of this device, try this experiment. Select someone you do not know well to participate with you, and ask them to stand about 10 feet away from you. Tell them you are going to move towards them and that their job involves letting you know the exact point at which they become uncomfortable with your closeness. Normally, this occurs at around three feet. Once you have done this, ask them to visualize a rose, to place it halfway between themselves and you, and to keep it there no matter how close you get. Then, try the exercise again with the instruction to the person to once more indicate when they become uncomfortable. You will find that you now can move much closer to them before they feel any discomfort. Holding the vision of the rose somehow prevents your energy from mixing with theirs.

The following forgiveness meditation uses the rose in a similar manner. It teaches you how to 'ground' energy, a wonderful method for bringing yourself into the present moment. You might want to record this meditation so you do not have to memorize it. Remember to speak it slowly into your recorder, leaving time for the images to come into your mind while you actually meditate. (Alternatively, you can order a pre-recorded tape of this meditation. See Appendix V.)

Sit comfortably in an upright chair with both feet flat on the floor. (This is important for grounding the energy.) Take three deep, long, relaxing breaths and close your eyes. Continue relaxing for a few moments, then visualize or imagine some kind of chord attached to the base of your spine and extending down through the floor into the earth and down into the center of the earth. It might be made of steel or rope, or it might be a solid structure. It might simply be a shaft of light. Whatever form it takes, this represents your attachment and connection to the planet Earth.

Now focus your awareness on the soles of your feet. You might notice a tingling sensation or some other sensation in that extremity. You might not feel anything unusual, and that is okay too. Feel, visualize or imagine energy beginning to move in through the soles of your feet, energy that comes from deep down in the Earth. Allow that energy to move slowly up your legs — from your heels to your knees — then into your thighs — up through the hips. See the energy flowing up from both legs until it meets at the base of the spine, at which point it travels back down the grounding chord to the center of the Earth again. Notice that this energy flows continually while you do this meditation and any time afterwards that you command your energy to flow in this manner.

Now imagine a ray of colored light coming from a Divine source out there in the cosmos. See the ray coming into your head through your crown chakra and filling the top half of your body with spiritual light and energy. You are totally connected to the energy of the Earth Mother and to the energy of Spirit. You are completely in balance now.

Now imagine a point behind your third eye, in the center of your forehead, halfway between your forehead and the back of your head, and halfway between either side of your head. Peace emanates from this point. Imagine yourself living in that spot and seeing the world from that point.

Now visualize or imagine a rose floating in front of you. Notice what color it is, what shape it takes and, perhaps, even how it smells. Notice too, that it is grounded to the center of the earth with a fine chord. With the rose still in front of you, begin to bring into your mind a picture of the person you wish to forgive. Allow the picture of the person to grow larger and clearer with every breath that you take. Notice the color of their hair, the texture of their skin, what they are wearing, the look on their face. Let everything about them become very clear in your mind. Notice any sounds they make or words they say, and hear them getting louder and louder. Hear the tone of the person's voice.

Bring the picture of the person a little bit closer to you, all the while keeping the rose between the two of you. Remember, the rose represents your complete protection, so no harm can come to you while the rose is there. As you look at the person through the image of the rose, become aware of what this person did to you that you want to forgive. Bring the person closer to the rose, very close in fact. In your mind, tell the person what he or she did to you and how you felt about it. Now allow the picture of the person to merge with the rose, and then see both images completely disintegrate in a flash of light.

Since the rose was grounded with a chord, the energy expended during the disintegration goes down the chord to the center of the Earth. In a few moments, allow the picture of the person and the rose to reform in your mind. Notice any slight difference in how the person looks. This time, tell the person: *"I am willing to pray for you."* Bring the person forward to merge with the rose, and have them disintegrate again in a flash of light. Feel the energy moving down the grounding chord attached to the rose into the center of the Earth.

Visualize the rose and the person once again. Notice an even greater change in how the person looks. Now tell the person: *"I am willing to forgive you."* If you only feel willing to forgive right now, that is fine. If you truly want to forgive, continue by saying: *"I am willing to forgive you, for I now realize that there was Divine purpose in the situation and I bless you for creating an opportunity for me to heal and to grow."* Bring the person and the rose together, and see them both disintegrate in the flash of light again.

Visualize the rose one more time, and see above you a great, golden sun. Reach your arms up into the golden rays, and allow the sun's warm energy to come down your arms into your whole body. Open your eyes and reach over and down until you can put your hands on the floor. Then stand up and stretch your arms once more into the golden sun. Relax.

Use this meditation in its full length when you have solitude and quiet, or use an abbreviated form while an event is happening. For example, if someone is trying to hurt you in some way, simply visualize the rose between you and that person. This provides a wonderful device for protecting you against negative energy. So, any time you feel someone is trying to control you or get into your energy field, put up your rose. You will find that you have the ability to retain your power and to be less affected by other people. If, in the moment, you stay conscious enough to bring them and the rose together and forgive them right there as you dissolve the rose and the picture into the light, you may even transform the event right in front of your eyes.

This process is a protective device yet it is not one that comes from fear. On the contrary, it allows us to engage a person more authentically and openly, for what the rose does is prevent a person from unconsciously either sucking our energy or manipulating us with their energy. The exchange is therefore cleaner and more real and gives us the opportunity to surrender to the other person at the soul level. Ultimately, all forgiveness is surrender. If you are able to surrender to another human being, even one who threatens you in some way, you will always be safe. The threat will evaporate. Nothing bad can happen to a truly surrendered person.

21: Seeing the Christ in Another

If you recognize that a situation occurring between you and someone else represents an opportunity to heal something in yourself, you can create the healing experience by being totally in that present moment. A way to bring your energy into present time, as opposed to allowing your mind to be in the past or in the future, requires simply looking at the person with whom you are having an issue and *seeing the Christ in them.*

In this sense, the term *Christ* means the part of them that is Divine and one with you and with God. As you do this, you join with them, and, in that moment, you acknowledge the Christ within you. If you have the presence of mind to do this, you will transform the situation immediately.

When we truly join with another person and become one with them, we transcend the Ego. The Ego's whole existence is based on separation. Without separation, we have no need to attack and defend — so in that moment of joining we raise our vibration, drop all our mechanisms of defense and become our true selves. At the same time we let go of our projections and see the other person as a child of God, perfect in every sense. This is the essence of Radical Forgiveness.

Seeing The Christ In Ourselves

It is important to recognize that the mechanism of projection does not just apply to the shadow side of us. We also project onto other people the things we like about ourselves yet have a hard time acknowledging. Thus we see in those people our own inner beauty, our own creative talent, our own intelligence and so on.

The Positive Reflection Exercise

This is an exercise taught by Arnold Patent and is powerful in its effect on everyone who tries it, because it asks you to see, first, what is wonderful in another person and, second, to claim that quality as your own. It truly connects people with their essence — with the Christ in themselves — and allows them to really see who they are. The exercise is usually done in a group setting, but it can equally be done with two people. It is similar to seeing the Christ in a person, but instead of doing it silently, this is done verbally and with eye contact.

Person A, speaking from the heart, says to person B, "The beautiful wonderful qualities that I see in you, that you reflect in me, are..." Person A, then tells the person the qualities they see. Person B, listens and responds by saying, "Thank you." They then switch over and repeat the exercise.

196

22: A Wake For Your Inner Child

Our spiritual evolution depends heavily upon our recovery from our worst addiction — our addiction to the victim archetype, which traps us in the past and saps our life energy. The inner child represents nothing but a metaphor for our woundedness and a *cutesy* form of victim consciousness. Wrapping our victim consciousness in baby clothes does not make it any more acceptable. Invoking our inner child still represents addictive behavior.

Please note, I am not talking about the playful, creative and life-affirming inner child, such as the one described by Richard Bach,* nor the part of ourselves that comes forward to inspire and to awaken us. I am talking about the whining little brat that lives in the back room of our mind, that unhappy victim who always can be relied upon to blame everyone else for our unhappiness. This is the one we pandered to at all those inner child workshops of the '80s.

For the sake of our spiritual evolution and of our eventual release from the victim archetype, we must bring the inner brat's life lovingly to a close. I, therefore, propose that you hold a funeral and pronounce him or her dead.

---

* Bach R. *"Running From Safety"* Morrow, 1994

If you choose to go ahead with this exercise, you will probably grieve the loss of your inner child, and that is okay. No doubt your inner child has given you solace and comfort in your pain over the years, but now it is time to move on. Radical Forgiveness releases you from the need to hold on to the woundedness, so allow yourself to release your inner child now.

As long as you hold on to your past wounds, Radical Forgiveness remains impossible. Holding onto your inner child only holds you back, because that child represents your past wounds. While you want to move on with your life, you may be surprised to find that your inner child may want to move on, too! To release your inner child, try the following meditation.

The Funeral Meditation

Sit comfortably, and take three deep breaths allowing your body to relax as your breath leaves your body. Notice any areas of your body that remain tight. Consciously relax them, knowing that during this meditation your body will continue to relax with every breath you take, and soon you will be profoundly relaxed from head to toe. Now look inside yourself and find the room in which sits the young person who has willingly carried your pain. Find the inner child who holds your memories of being abused, ignored, betrayed, abandoned, unaccepted, unloved.

As you come upon this little person in that room, notice that he or she is surrounded by ledgers and score lists.

The walls of the room are covered with people's names, what they did to you and what punishment they deserve. In the ledgers, the child keeps a careful tally of all the times someone victimized you and what it cost you. Notice the joylessness of this room. As you look at this young child, realize how sad he or she really feels locked down there alone with the pain, mired down in victim consciousness.

Realizing that it is time for a change, you walk across the room and throw open the windows to let in the light. As the sun floods into the room, the ink on the wall charts starts to fade and the books start to crumble and become dust. The lists on the wall also fall to the ground and crumble. Look at the little person who has lived in this room for all those years keeping resentment scores day by day. See his or her broad smile and joyous expression.

"Now I am free to go," the child says.

"Go where?" you ask.

"I'm free to go to the next place. I should have left years ago, but I've been waiting for you to release me from this job."

Suddenly you notice that this person, who was young and child-like such a short while ago, is growing old and becoming wizened and grey-haired right before your eyes. Yet, a great peace has replaced his or her sadness. "Thank you for letting me go," he/she gasps, lying down slowly on a couch."

You say, "I'm sorry it's taken so long to bring light into this room. I'm sorry I've held you back."

"That's quite alright," comes the quiet reply. "It really is okay. Time is just an illusion anyway. Goodbye." With that, the little person dies, looking peaceful and serene.

Lovingly, you wrap the little person in a white cloth and take the body upstairs and out into the light. There waits a horse and buggy, and angels hover nearby. A choir of angels sings softly. All the people who have ever been in your life are waiting to pay their respects. All past hurts are forgiven. Love is everywhere. The bells on the horse and buggy ring softly as the entourage slowly begins its journey to the hill where a grave has been prepared. At the graveside, everyone sings and great joy envelops the group. Your angels are with you and support you as you say your last farewell. See the little person being lowered lovingly and gently into the grave as the celestial choir sings. As a stone is moved over the grave, you feel a new sense of freedom and love moving through you.

You walk to the bottom of the hill where you find a fast running stream. You wash your hands and your face in the water and see your reflection in the water. You feel the cleansing water of the stream running through your being, taking with it all the dust and debris from the room where the little person once dwelt. Hear the sound of the water babbling over the rocks. See the sun sparkling on the water, and feel the warmth of the sun on your body. Notice the green of the surrounding fields and the many bright flowers around. All is well. Open your eyes whenever you feel ready.

Being without your wounded inner child will feel strange for a while, but you also will begin to notice some positive changes. You will feel lighter, less burdened, more in the moment. Your life energy will increase as you retrieve the energy that previously was spent holding on to the wounds of the inner child.

Be prepared to encounter problems with close friends with whom you previously spent time sharing wounds. They will not like the change in you, for they will see that you no longer give your wounds power. Since they remain committed to their wounds, they may be uncomfortable with you; they may even begin feeling as if you have betrayed them. If you are member of a support group that thrives on the sharing of wounds, such as Adult Children of Alcoholics (ACOA) or Incest Survivors, be prepared to disconnect yourself from the group. You probably will find your need to attend group meetings diminishing anyway, but, if you are the least bit co-dependent, you might still feel as if leaving the group is a challenge. Stick to your guns, and do not take other people's attempts to disconnect from you or talk of betrayal personally. These people will come around eventually and probably will want some of what they see you have gained.

23: Forgiveness Is A 3-Letter Word

The 'Trilogy of Letters' provides a good tool to use when in a highly charged emotional state about a situation. It works wonderfully when you are really upset either about something that has just happened or something that might have happened a long time ago.

This tool simply involves writing three letters to the person you feel has wronged or hurt you in some way. First, vent all your anger and rage in a letter to that person. Hold nothing back. You can threaten vengeance of the vilest kind if it makes you feel good. Keep writing until you have nothing left to say. The process of writing this letter may cause you to shed a lot of tears — tears of rage, sadness, resentment, and hurt. Let them flow. Have a box of tissues beside you. If you are angry, scream into a pillow or do any of the other exercises mentioned in Chapter 13 to help you feel your anger. *Under no circumstances mail this letter!*

The next day, write another letter. This one should carry somewhat less anger and vengeance, although it still does not let the person with whom you are angry off the hook for what you believe they have done to you. However, it should make an effort to bring compassion, understanding, and generosity, as well as the possibility of some sort of forgiveness, into the equation. ***Do not mail this letter either.***

The following day, write a third letter. In this one, attempt to describe a new interpretation of the situation based on the principles of Radical Forgiveness. Since this mimics the forgiveness worksheet, refer to the notes on the worksheet to give you the signposts for your letter, but write it in your own words as best you can. (See Chapter 29.) This may feel like a struggle at first, but persevere. Remember, you will have to fake it for a while before you make it.

None of these letters are ever mailed. It is neither necessary nor desirable to mail them. They are designed to shift *your* energy, not the energy of the recipient. Venting your feelings, rather than projecting them once again onto the other person serves as the objective. Sending the angry letter, in particular, accomplishes nothing whatsoever. Doing so would only keep the attack-defense cycle going on and on, and that would drag you deeper into the drama. Remember, as you shift your energy in the direction of Radical Forgiveness, the energy of the other person changes automatically.

You either can keep the letters for future reference, or you can use them in a forgiveness ritual. My personal preference lies in using the ritual of fire to transform them. Something powerful happens when you see your words turned into ashes and rise up in a column of smoke.

24: Forgiveness Rituals

The power of ritual is underestimated in our society today. When we ritualize any procedure we make it sacred, thus the ritual speaks directly to our soul. While rituals can be very simple or quite complex, the complexity matters less than the reverence you show the ritual. The ritual invites the participation of the Divine in human affairs and, as such, represents another way of praying.

Rituals become all the more powerful when we create them ourselves. When devising your own rituals, be as creative as you can. However, here are some general guidelines and ideas you may want to use.

Ritual With Fire

Fire has always been the element of transformation and alchemy. Whenever we offer something up through fire, we tap into primordial beliefs in fire's transformative power. For this reason, a ritual burning of a forgiveness worksheet, a release letter or the letter trilogy provides a sense of completion and transformation. Carry out the burning with ceremony and with reverence. Say a prayer as the item burns.

Burning scented woods, sage, sweetgrass, and incense will intensify any ritual and bring special significance to a forgiveness ceremony. The smoke from sage and sweet grass also cleanses your aura; thus removing unwanted energies from your energy field.

Ritual With Water

Water possesses healing and cleansing qualities, and we give it the ability to make things holy. Ritualized washing, immersing and floating all can be used to good effect. For example, instead of burning a release letter, fold it into a boat and let a fast flowing stream of water take it away.

Be creative with your rituals, and make them meaningful to you. You may recall the story of Jane who had brain cancer and had put in the attic a box containing everything associated with a man who broke her heart. I asked her to take the box down from the attic and bring it with her to therapy. Had she not had a seizure and died before we could do so, we would have gone through the box examining every item in it and what it meant to her. Then, we would have disposed of them one by one with a ritual bearing meaning for her. This process would have released much repressed energy.

25: Artful Forgiveness

Art provides a powerful tool for forgiveness and emotional release. One of the most dramatic healings through art I have ever been privileged to witness and/or to participate in, occurred at a retreat I did in England. One of the participants was a young woman with multiple sclerosis. Her body was weak and wasted, and her voice was hardly audible. Her throat chakra was virtually shut down. She had a husband and two children, but the marriage was basically non-existent and she felt trapped, helpless and hopeless.

At one point during a group art therapy session, she began to draw in a particularly unique fashion. She could not talk, but she kept drawing and drawing. It was hard to discern what she was drawing, but it became clear over time that she was using the medium as a way to regress herself and release old childhood pain.

My wife and I sat there with her as she drew hour after hour, her drawings becoming more and more child-like as time went on. In addition to her pictures, occasionally she would scrawl phrases like, *bad girl,* and *God doesn't love me,* and other words indicating deep shame, guilt and fear. Finally, she made a crude stick drawing of what she later re-called as childhood rape by an uncle. In this cathartic release, she was able to express in drawings what she had found it impossible to say in words and sounds. Her throat chakra had shut down because of what she was forced to do with her mouth. (Her uncle had made her have oral sex with him.) Suddenly, art became an outlet for memories and emotions that had remained repressed for many years. These memories and emotions were responsible for her illness.

To support this woman in her catharsis, my wife went to the far end of the rather large room in which we were holding the retreat. We then asked her to use her voice to tell my wife that she was a *good girl,* and that *God loved her.* I make her do it louder and louder until she was shouting at the top of her lungs. After she had shouted, *God loves me,* about 20 times, she stopped and looked at me and affirmed, "He really does love me, doesn't he!" That healing moment I will never forget.

Three months after we got back from England, we received a letter from her say she had left her husband, had gotten a new place to live and had found a job. She was using her voice and asking for what she wanted, and she was finding that she had the power, not only to ask, but also to receive. She had even started a support group for people with multiple sclerosis and was doing art therapy with them. Her strength was returning day by day, and, after three years, we still hear from her and marvel at her continuously increasing strength.

If you are not a verbally inclined person and are not comfortable writing things down, try drawing. You may be
surprised what will happen when you communicate in this
manner. Buy some decently sized white and black paper
as well as some colored pastel chalks and crayons. (The
pastels work really well on the black paper.)

Know that to use this tool requires no artistic talent whatsoever. It is not about painting pretty pictures. In fact, if
you are full of anger, your pictures will probably be anything but pretty. It is about getting emotions and thoughts
out on paper.

Begin drawing with no expectations or pre-conceived ideas.
You might ask God or your spirit guides to help you release through the process of drawing and coloring whatever needs releasing, and then simply start. Whatever
wants to come, allow it. Do not judge. Just go with the
flow. Do this like a meditation. If you want to tell a story,
do that. If you just want to use color, do that. Do whatever you feel like doing.

To use art therapy as a forgiveness tool, use an approach
similar to that of the letter trilogy. Do a series of drawings
that express how you felt about what a particular person
did to you; these pictures would express your anger, fear,
pain, sadness, etc. Then, move into mock forgiveness with
a more compassionate and understanding frame of mind,
and do some drawings that reflect this attitude. Do a third
set that expresses the feeling of Radical Forgiveness. You
might want to put some time between each phase, or you

can do them all in the same sitting. Make sure, however, that once you start doing this art therapy, you complete all three stages — even if you only do three drawings in all. Doing just the first one, for example, might leave you stuck in anger.

As you finish each picture, hang it on a wall. Place each picture in the precise order in which you complete them, and create a vertical or horizontal band on the wall with them. If you are creating a vertical display, begin with the first of the angry ones at the bottom and end with the last Radical Forgiveness one at the top. When you place them in such a manner, you will be amazed to see the progression and the change in the quality of the energy expressed by each picture.

Title each drawing and date it. Spend some time with the drawings. Let them "speak" to you. While you were drawing each picture, you were thinking certain thoughts. When you look at the drawing later, clear your mind of those thoughts and examine the pictures for anything else of importance. Invite others you trust to give you their interpretations of the pictures. They may see things you do not. Ask for their input by saying, "If this were your picture, what would you see?" If what they see resonates with you, fine. If it does not really ring true for you, that is fine too. They see into your drawing through their own subconscious, not yours, but you will find that people's observations will trigger within you a whole new way of looking at your drawings, and you may have some new insights as a result.

Two doctors attended the first cancer retreat we ever held. They were man and wife. She had had breast cancer and was an internist. He was there to support her and worked as a family practitioner. They both did a tremendous amount of painting and got fresh insights every day. He, in particular, found that expressing himself through drawing provided an incredible release. He was a man who did not verbalize his feelings much. Suddenly, through drawing, he found a powerful way of expressing emotions that felt safe as well as powerful. Symbols on paper became extremely meaningful to him and, once on paper, he could articulate exactly what was going on for him. He spent one of the days at the retreat in total silence doing nothing but drawing.

26: Satori Breathwork

As we have discussed previously, suppressed or repressed emotions have toxic effects on both our mental and physical health. Releasing these emotions serves as the first step in the forgiveness process. We can release held emotions the most quickly and the most effectively by using a process called Satori Breath. (Satori is a Sanskrit word meaning 'insight.')

Satori breathwork is usually done lying on your back and involves breathing with full awareness in a circular pattern. In other words, you consciously breathe in a manner that has no pause between the in-breath and the out-breath. Carefully selected music is played rather loudly throughout the process.

The person breathes for between 40 to 60 minutes through an open mouth, sometimes long and deep into the abdomen, and at other times fast and shallow into the upper chest. This oxygenates the body to such an extent that the body releases from its cells suppressed emotion that has crystallized into energy particles within the cells. As these energy particles are released, the person often becomes consciously aware of these old feelings in present time.

The feelings may be expressed as pure emotion, such as sadness, anger or despair, unattached to any memory associated with them. Conversely, the memory of an event, idea, association or misperception that caused the emotion to be felt and suppressed in the first place may come sharply into focus. It may even surface in a symbolic way or in the form of a metaphor. On the other hand, there may be no conscious recall of anything. For each person and in each breathing session, the experience is different as well as impossible to predict.

As emotions come up, the person *breathes through* them, which allows the person not only to feel them fully but to release them. We often stop breathing to hold emotions in check; therefore, breathing through them allows us to feel them and release them. In some cases, the person expresses them verbally and kinesthetically while breathing. No matter how the emotions are released, almost invariably a sense of profound calm and deep peace results from the process.

This simple technique provides dramatic and long-lasting healing effects. I have no hesitation in recommending this work to anyone who is serious about wanting to clear out their emotional closet.

The effects of Satori Breathwork are profound precisely because they happen totally within the person without any interjection, guidance, steering, or manipulation whatsoever by the facilitator. In fact, a facilitator only is present to *hold the space as safe* and to support the breather in moving through the feelings — which sometimes can be scary — rather than suppressing them again. I would not recommend that you do this process on your own for that reason.

Conscious connected breathing is also called *rebirthing,* because researchers have found that breathwork gives us access to memories and emotions lodged in our cells as early as during our in-utero experience, during the actual birth process and soon after the birth. Birth represents our first major life trauma, and we form profound ideas about struggle, abandonment, safety and acceptance as we go through this experience. These ideas often become beliefs that literally run our lives. When someone re-experiences their birth and releases the traumas and beliefs they formed at that time, their lives change dramatically.

Another great benefit of Satori Breathwork comes from the fact that it integrates new energy patterns into our existing energy fields and restructures our subtle bodies accordingly. This means that when you shift your perception, have an insight or release old emotional patterns, breathwork integrates this into your body's data banks. Using the computer analogy, it is as if breathwork serves as a downloading process where data currently stored in the short-term computer memory is transferred to the hard drive for permanent storage.

This also explains why Satori Breathwork becomes so important in the Radical Forgiveness process. It accomplishes these tasks, not just at the beginning of the process for the purpose of emotional release, but afterwards too, when our belief systems change and all the resulting changes in our energy fields need integrating. The integration process anchors the changes in our bodies and helps prevent us from going back to our old ways.

I would suggest that you have between 10 and 20 supervised breathing sessions over a period of time, which may take up to a year. After that, you can probably do the breathing process on your own.

27: "Pray For The S.O.B."

All forgiveness is prayer. We cannot *will* forgiveness nor control when we achieve it. Asking for the support of God, the Universe, Higher Intelligence, Jesus, whomever, to bring us to the point of forgiveness provides the foundation for all the tools in this section. Yet, it makes sense to isolate the activity of prayer as a tool in its own right, if only as a reminder of its profundity and of the fact that it provides this foundation.

Nowhere is the power of prayer better understood than in Alcoholics Anonymous (AA) nor more straightforwardly conveyed. When a person approaches an AA sponsor or friend to complain of being victimized or to moan that he cannot rid himself of a resentment because he feels *unable to forgive*, the following advice is often judiciously offered: "Pray for the s.o.b!"

Astounding as it may sound to an outsider, it works! Time after time at AA meetings people relate experiences of forgiveness achieved through prayer. "I just couldn't forgive him, but my sponsor said, 'Pray for the s.o.b., and I did. And, would you believe it? One day I realized I no longer felt resentful... somehow, the whole thing just didn't bother me anymore!"

As Ernest Kurtz and Katherine Ketcham point out, "The prayer that usually works is the only prayer often possible. 'God, please give that s.o.b. what he deserves!' And as long as one does not presume to suggest *what he deserves,* amazingly, it works."*

This brings us to a key point about prayer: Implicit in all prayer lies surrender of our claim to control the outcome. Often our prayers boss the Universe around, and tell God exactly what He should, or should not, do for us, as if we presumed to know better than He what was truly in our highest and best interest. Such prayers rarely achieve the desired results.

In our prayers for forgiveness, whether they come from the perspective of Mock Forgiveness, as do the above examples, or Radical Forgiveness, all we need do is ask for help. When we come from a Radical Forgiveness perspective, we can be more specific and ask for help in seeing the perfection in the situation, in joining with the person, in taking back the projection, and so on.

Individual prayer serves as a powerful tool, but enlisting the help of others in praying on our behalf enhances the effects of this tool. Some quite respectable scientific studies have proven the power of prayer to heal, especially when many people pray together for that healing.

Many people use the MasterMind approach. This works

Kurtz E., & Ketcham, K., *"The Spirituality of Imperfection"* Bantam Books, 1994

on the biblical principle of *whenever two or more are gath*ered in my name... and involves a group of people committed to meeting regularly for the purpose of jointly asking the Master Mind (God) for help in certain matters. Help in forgiving someone would be a typical request of a participant in such a group. Thousands of people attend such groups on a weekly or bi-weekly basis and report extraordinary success.

28: The Release Letter

The Release Letter is an adaptation of a letter given to me by hypnotherapist and mind/body therapist, Dr. Sharon Forrest of the Forrest Foundation, a non profit corporation dedicated to alternative holistic healing, located in Mexico.

The Release Letter proclaims to your Higher Self and to every part of your being that you give full permission for all aspects of unforgiveness still remaining in any situation to be lovingly released.

It also serves as an instrument of self-forgiveness, for it recognizes that you have created the experiences as a way to learn and to grow.

Photocopy the letter as written on the following page and enlarge to an appropriate size. Alternatively, send for the plastic laminated Release Letter as part of the package of forgiveness worksheets. (See Appendix V).

To use the Release Letter, fill in the blanks, have it witnessed by someone and then burn it in a ritual manner.

Release Letter

Date: _____ Name _____

Dear Higher Self:

I, _____ , hereby grant you, my Higher Self, my Soul, my Super-Conscious Mind, my DNA, my cellular memory, and all parts of myself that might want to hold onto the unforgiveness for whatever reason, to release all of the misunderstandings, unfounded beliefs, misinterpretations, unfounded beliefs, misinterpretations and misguided emotions, wherever they may reside, whether in my body, my unconscious mind, my DNA, my conscious mind, my subconsious mind, my unconscious mind, my chakras and even my Soul, and I ask all those who want the best for me to assist in this releasing process.

I, _____ , thank you, my Soul, for creating the experiences that created the unforgiveness and realize that on some level they have all been my teachers and have offered me opportunites for me to learn and to grow. I accept the experiences, without judgment and do hereby release them to the nothingness from which they came.

I, _____ , do hereby forgive _____

I release him/her to their highest good and set him/her free. I bless him/her for having been willing to be my teacher. I sever all unhealthy attachments to this person and send him/her unconditional love and support.

I, _____ , do hereby forgive myself, and accept myself just the way I am and love myself unconditionally just the way I am, in all my power and magnificence.

I, _____ , do hereby release myself to my highest good and claim for myself freedom, fulfilment of my dreams, wishes and goals, clarity, love, full expression, creativity, health and prosperity.

Signed: _____ Date: _____

Witnessed by: _____ Date: _____

29: Making Room for the Miracle

The Radical Forgiveness worksheet is, in my opinion, the most transformational tool in this book. It has literally changed people's lives. It is not easy to explain how and why it accomplishes such dramatic results except to say that it helps people shift their energy. In fact, you could say that doing the worksheet is, in and of itself, an energy experience.

It should be clear to you by now that, any time anyone upsets you or triggers negative emotion, its your *stuff*. Where before you would have been sucked into the drama, now you can reach for a worksheet and start the forgiveness process.

Keep doing worksheets until the energy around the situation, person or incident dissipates. This could take days or months. On the other hand, maybe just one worksheet will produce the desired result. It all depends on what is being resonated and the depth of the emotion being triggered. For this reason, both a long and a short version of the worksheet have been provided. Always use the longer worksheet the first two or three times you complete one; after that you can switch to the short form.

Making Room for The Miracle

A Radical Forgiveness Worksheet

Date: ▓▓▓▓   Worksheet # ▓▓▓   Subject: (X) *Whomever or whatever you are upset about:* ▓▓▓▓▓▓▓▓▓▓▓▓

1. The situation as I perceive it now is:

BREATHE

Confronting Subject (X)

2a) I am upset because:

2b) I am feeling: *(Idenity your __real__ emotions here).*

2c) I think: *(Identify the thoughts attached to the emotions).*

3. I lovingly recognize and accept my feelings, *(as in 2b)* without judgment, of:

I own my feelings. No-one can make me feel anything. My feelings are a reflection of my consciousness around the situation.

4. Even though I do not know why, I recognize that I have created this situation in order that I can learn and grow. *(Comment on this and attempt a possible explanation for why you may have created the situation).*

5. FIVE INSIGHTS IN RADICAL FORGIVENESS: AFFIRM NOW.

a. When I feel uncomfortable, I know there is a part of me that needs to be healed. (X) ▓▓▓▓▓▓▓▓ is reflecting this for me so that I can see what I need to forgive in myself.

b. I now realize that I get upset only when someone resonates in me what I have denied, repressed and projected onto others. The situation is a precise mirror of my consciousness around this issue.

c. I now realize that the way I see (X) is precisely the way I unconsciously see myself. In forgiving (X), I forgive myself.

d. I appreciate your willingness (x) ▓▓▓▓▓▓▓▓▓▓ to mirror my misperceptions, and I bless you for providing me with the opportunity to practice Radical Forgiveness and heal.

e. I now see that I am a spiritual being having a human experience, and I forgive my Ego for using guilt, anger, blame and judgment to lower my vibration and keep me separated from the World of DivineTruth.

6. I now realize that nothing (X), or anyone else, has done is either right or wrong. I drop all judgment. I release the need to blame and the need to be right and I recognize the perfection in the situation just the way it is. *(Comment truthfully on this.)*

7. My discomfort was my signal that I was witholding love from myself and others. *(Describe how you were witholding love)*

Acknowledgements: Dr. Michael Ryce and Arnold M. Patent.

The two worksheets are included in Appendix II in case you want to cut them out so you can photocopy them and enlarge them. (Better yet, you can order full-size laminated copies of both worksheets and the Release Letter, by turning to the order form in Appendix V).

The detailed instructions and *coaching notes* on each step of the worksheet are given below. The relevant parts of the worksheet are highlighted and, by way of example, *filled in* as *if Jill had completed it at the time she was going through the situation with Jeff* (See Part One, Chapter One).

Completing the worksheet requires a firm grasp of the principles underlying Radical Forgiveness and the following *notes* serve as a reminder of them. If you experience difficulty with any part of the worksheet, review Parts Two and Three of this book.

When we start with Radical Forgiveness, we have a tendency to want to do too many worksheets on too many people from our list, and to work immediately with the major issues of the past. However, one of Radical Forgiveness' best characteristics lies in the fact that we do not have to dig up the past to heal it. Whomever is upsetting you *right now,* is the person who represents ALL the people who have ever upset you for the same reason in the past. So work with that person first, even if you're thinking that it's no big deal. If it's upsetting you, it *is* a big deal. It could easily lead you to what really matters.

You might want to start with the smaller issues; ones that

are fairly simple and without a great deal of emotional charge. Small problems grow into big ones if they are not dealt with, so you will be doing important work even with seemingly trivial situations. Besides that, it is much easier to learn how to create the necessary shifts in perception with simpler, less traumatic situations. Leave the big ones for later.

It is important to date and number these sheets and then file them. This allows you to review them from time to time and to evaluate the extent to which your consciousness has changed.

Special Acknowledgments

These worksheets have their origins in a forgiveness worksheet created some years ago by Dr. Michael Ryce, a pioneer in this field and one who has dedicated his life to bringing the message of forgiveness to everyone on the planet, and in the work of Arnold M. Patent. Arnold originally introduced me to spiritual principle and his work inspires many of the steps in this forgiveness worksheet. In the shorter worksheet I wish to acknowledge the additional influence of Caroline Myss and 'Abraham.' I am deeply grateful for the contributions each have made to my understanding and, by extension, to this book.

Making Room For The Miracle
A Radical Forgiveness Worksheet

Date: **8/7/91**   Worksheet #   **3**

Subject (X) Whomever or whatever you are upset about   **JEFF**

• Identify the person, situation or object about which you feel upset, here noted as "X." This may even be yourself. Be sure to write about him/her/it/yourself in the third person context. In other words use names. If the object or situation has no name, give it one. Personify an object, and then write about it, speak to it, as if it were a person. If the person happens to be dead, speak to them in the present tense as if you have direct contact with them.

---

1. The Situation as I perceive it now is:

Jeff is abandoning me by focussing all his attention and love on his daughter Lorraine -- completely ignoring me. He makes me wrong and accuses me of being mentally unbalanced. He makes me feel worthless and stupid. Our marriage is over and its all his fault. He is forcing me to leave him.

---

1. This section asks you to tell the story about your upset. Define the situation. Do not hold back. Describe how it feels for you right now. Do not edit or overlay it with any spiritual or psychological interpretation. You must honor where you are now, even if you know that you are in the World of Humanity, Ego and illusion. Knowing that you are experiencing illusion, and that you need to experience it, represents the first step toward escaping from it.

Even if we have raised our vibration considerably and spend a fair bit of our lives in the World of Divine Truth, we can easily be knocked off balance and find ourselves back in the world of Ego seeing ourselves as victims and all that goes with that. Being human requires that experience. We cannot always be joyful and peaceful and see the perfection in absolutely every situation.

Breathe

• Notice when you stop breathing. Holding our breath denotes resistance. Breathing acts like a switch that turns our energy, our openness to experiencing our feelings, on or off. To maintain the open or "ON" position, consciously decide to breathe. Breathing deeply from the stomach keeps the energy flowing.

---

2.   Confronting Subject (X)

(a) **I am upset because:**

You have ruined our marriage. You have hurt me and rejected me. Your behavior stinks!

2a. Be as confrontive as possible with X, and lay out exactly what you blame him/her/it for. This section's small space only allows a few words, but let the words you choose represent the totality of your upset. If you want to write it out in full, do so in the form of a letter. (See Chapter 23.) This step allows you to address the person directly. However, keep to one issue. Do not discuss other things in the letter, or on this worksheet. Reaching your objective — Radical Forgiveness — requires you to get clarity on precisely what you feel so upset about *now*.

(b) **I am feeling.**: *(Identify your real emotions here)*

Deeply hurt, abandoned, betrayed. I feel very alone and sad. You've made me angry.

2b. It is vitally important that you allow yourself to feel your feelings. Do not censor them or *stuff* them. Remember, we came into the physical realm to experience emotion — the essence of being human. All emotions are good, except when we suppress them. Stuffing emotion creates potentially harmful energy blocks in our bodies.

Make sure the emotions you identify represent real emotions that you actually feel, not just *thoughts* about how you feel. Are you *mad, glad, sad,* or *afraid*? If you cannot be specific, that is okay. Some people find themselves unable to differentiate one feeling from another. If that holds true for you, just notice what general emotional quality you can feel around the situation.

If you would like to feel your emotions more clearly or strongly, pick up a tennis racquet or a bat and beat the heck out of some cushions or pillows. Use something that will make a noise when you hit the cushions. If anger scares you, have someone with you when you do this exercise. That person should encourage and support you in feeling your anger (or any other emotion) and make it safe to do so. Screaming into a cushion also helps release feelings. As we stressed in Chapter 16, the more you allow yourself to feel the hurt, sadness or fear that might lie beneath your anger, the better.

(c) **I think:** (Identify the thoughts attached to the emotions:)

You act like this just to hurt me and make feel worthless. You have betrayed me.

2c. You likely will arrive at this section's contents while completing the previous one, "I am feeling," because an emotion is *a thought attached to a feeling.* The thought behind the emotion identifies the source of your pain and hurt and stirs up the anger within you. Typical thoughts might be, "You betrayed me...I thought I could trust you. You abandoned me. I gave you everything and then...you lied to me." Or your thought might begin with the phrase "It wasn't right that..." When you allow such thoughts to come into your consciousness, tears often begin to flow. Let them flow. Tears cleanse and heal.

> **3.** I recognize and lovingly accept my feelings, without judgment, of:
>
> ## *Anger, sadness, hurt, frustration.*
>
> I own my feelings. No-one can MAKE me feel anything. My feelings are a reflection of my consciousness around the situation.

3. This important step provides you with an opportunity to allow yourself some self-love and appreciation. You may need to spend a few moments in meditation before completing this section. You need to feel your emotions in exactly the way they occur for you, for they are an expression of your true self. Your soul wants you to feel them fully. Know they are perfect.

Try the following three-step process for integrating and accepting your feelings:

1. Feel the feeling fully, and then identify it as either mad, glad, sad, or afraid.

2. Embrace the feelings in your heart just the way they are. *Love them. Accept them.* Love them as part of yourself. Let them be perfect You cannot move into the joy vibration without first accepting your feelings and making peace with them. Say this affirmation: *"I ask for support in feeling love for each of my emotions just the way it is, as I embrace it within my heart and accept it lovingly as part of myself."*

3. Now *feel love for yourself* for having these feelings and know you have chosen to feel them as a way of moving your energy towards healing.

Read the statement at the bottom of the box: *"I own my feelings. No one can make me feel anything. My feelings are a reflection of my consciousness around this situation."* This statement reminds us that no-one can make us feel anything. Our emotions are our own. As we feel, recognize, accept, and love them unconditionally as part of ourselves, we become entirely free to hold on to them or let them go. This realization empowers us by helping us realize that the problem resides not *out there* but *in here*, within ourselves. This realization also represents our first step away from the victim archetype vibration. When we think other people, or even situations, make us mad, glad, sad, or afraid, we give them all our power.

If you are experiencing less than love and joy, you are out of alignment with your Divine essence. You are caught in misperceptions. Your feelings are perfect feedback to remind you that you created the situation to learn and to grow.

---

4. Even though I do not know why, I recognize that I have created this situation in order to learn and to grow. *(Attempt an explanation)*

It's hard for me to really understand what is going on but I am trying to see how Jeff is showing me my core belief that I am not loveable or 'not-enough,' and that in doing so, he is really giving me unconditional love. My soul has created this situation in

---

> *order to give me the chance to see how I have*
> *created myself as 'not-enough' all through my life.*
> *This is my chance to heal that belief.*

4. This statement reminds us of the Law of Cause and Effect. It reinforces the notion that thoughts, feelings and beliefs create our experiences and that, furthermore, we order our reality in such a way as to support our spiritual growth. When we open ourselves to this truth, the problem almost always disappears. That's because there are no problems, only misperceptions.

This section then challenges us to see the perfection in the situation and to write something acknowledging this. We may not find it easy to see the perfection, and we may find ourselves face to face with our resistance to seeing it this way and to letting go of the victim archetype.

The Ego always tries to make us focus entirely on what we project outside of ourselves. It wants us to believe we are victimized by others and that to be happy we only need change the external world.

The importance of this step comes in its ability to help you feel your way out of the victim mode into the possibility that the person, object or situation with whom you have the issue reflects precisely that part of yourself that you have rejected and which cries out to be accepted. It acknowledges that the Divine essence within, the knowing part of yourself, your soul — whatever you want to call it, has set the situation up for you, so you can learn, grow and heal a misperception or a false belief.

This step also creates self-empowerment. Once we realize we have created a situation, we have the power to change it. We can choose to see ourselves as the victim of circumstance, or we can choose to see our circumstance as an opportunity to learn and to grow and to have our lives be the way we want.

Do not judge yourself for creating a situation. Remember, the Divine part of yourself created it. If you judge the Divine part of you, you judge God. Acknowledge yourself as a wonderful, creative, Divine being with the ability to create your own lessons along the spiritual path, lessons that eventually will take you home. Once you are able to do this, you are able to surrender to the Divine essence that you are and to trust it to do the rest.

---

5. FIVE INSIGHTS:

a. When I feel uncomfortable, I know there is a part of me that needs to be healed. (X) *Jeff* is reflecting this for me so I can see what I need to forgive in myself.

5a. This first of these five insights acknowledges that our bodies act like an antenna. When someone *pushes our buttons* — does something that creates an emotional response within us, the emotion manifests as discomfort in our body. This discomfort provides a signal that indicates we are out of alignment with truth, our energy is blocked and something needs to be healed. You can feel grateful to X for resonating with your energy block in an attempt to bring it to your attention. By forgiving X, you forgive yourself, (take back the projection) and the energy used for projecting is freed to move through you.

> **b.** I now realize that I get upset only when someone resonates in me what I have repressed, denied and projected onto others. It is a precise mirror of my consciousness around this issue.

5b. This insight connects us again with the principle dealt with in step #4. Value exists in continuing to confront this principle until we understand it at the feeling level. It also reminds us of the Law of Attraction, which mandates that we attract people, objects or situations into our lives that acquaint us with what we have denied, repressed or projected onto others. We also become empowered when we realize that what we attack and judge in others represents precisely what we condemn in ourselves.

> **c.** I now realize that the way I see (X) *Jeff* is really the way I unconsciously see myself. In forgiving him/her, I forgive myself.

5c. With this insight we retract the projection and express acceptance of that part of ourselves we have denied.

> **d.** I appreciate your willingness (X) *Jeff* to mirror my misperceptions and I bless you for providing the opportunity to practice Radical Forgiveness.

5d. Spend some moments meditating on this insight that has created in you a deep feeling of appreciation for X.

> **e.** I now realize that I am a spiritual being having a human experience and I forgive my Ego for using guilt, anger, blame and judgment to keep me separated from the world of Divine Truth.

5e. The belief that we are spiritual beings having a human experience is gaining wide acceptance. As such, it represents a profound shift in spiritual awareness, for it clearly means that, far from being in exile from God we are at home in The World of Divine Truth, and only on this earth plane temporarily. Understanding this truth represents a giant step in our spiritual evolution, and makes the Ego very uneasy. The Ego wants us to feel permanently disconnected from God and in constant danger of punishment for the original sin. In fact, the Ego's survival depends on us feeling this way.

> **6.** I now realize that nothing (X) (or anyone else), has done, can be either right or wrong. I drop all judgments. I release the need to blame and the need to be right, and I recognize the perfection in the situation just the way it is. *(Comment truthfully on this)*
>
> *I am trying to see that nothing that is happening is either right or wrong, good or bad. It's hard, but I am willing to look for their being a divine plan unfolding here and that I am being lovingly supported in a healing process by everyone involved.*

6. This step confronts you with the perfection in the situation and tests your ability to really see this perfection. While it never will be easy to see the perfection or good in something such as child abuse, we can be *willing* to see the perfection in the situation, be *willing* to drop the judgement and be *willing to drop the need to be right*. While it may always be difficult to recognize that both the abuser and the abused somehow created their situation to learn a lesson at the soul level, and that their mission was to transform the situation on behalf of all abused people, we can nevertheless be *willing* to entertain this thought.

Obviously, the closer we are to a situation, the more difficult it becomes to see its perfection, but seeing the perfection does not always mean understanding it. We cannot always know the reasons why things happen as they do; we must simply have faith that they are happening perfectly and for the highest good of all.

Observe your strong need to be right. We possess an enormous investment in being right and we learned at an early age to fight to be right, which usually means proving that someone else is wrong. We even measure our self worth by how often we are right, thus it is no wonder that we have such trouble accepting that something just *is* — that it is neither inherently right nor wrong.

When you notice yourself invested in being right in any given situation, recognize that you are projecting your guilt and fear and that you are disconnected from your Divine wisdom. As you release that need and surrender to what *is* — to the actual situation without your judgement-based bias making it either wrong or right, you will become more peaceful and aligned.

As you write your comment in this section, be true to yourself. If you really cannot at this point drop your judgment about something that seems awful, just reconnect with your feelings (see step #3 above), move into them and admit to yourself that you cannot yet take this step. However, *be willing* to drop your judgment. Willingness remains the key. As the energy changes, all else follows.

---

7. My discomfort is my signal that I am (or was) withholding love from myself and others. *(Describe how you were withholding love).*

I realize that my committment was to making Jeff wrong and blaming him for my discomfort - when really I was responsible for it all the time. I was withholding love from him and myself by not recognizing the truth — that I am loved. I was not letting that love in. I was judging myself and others and blinding myself to the reality of God's love for me.

---

7. When we feel disconnected from someone, we cannot love them. When we judge a person (or ourselves) and make them wrong, we withhold love. Even when we make them right, we are withholding love, because we make our love conditional upon their *rightness* continuing.

238

Any attempt to change someone involves a withdrawal of love, because wanting them to change implies that they are wrong (need to change) in some way. Furthermore, we may even do harm in encouraging them to change, for though we may act with the best intentions, we may interfere with their spiritual lesson, mission and advancement.

Note: It is at this point that you turn the worksheet over to work from its second side. Please make a ritual of turning it over, because as you do so, you symbolically move from the World of Humanity, Ego and Illusion (represented by all the questions on the front side of the sheet) to the world of Divine Truth (represented by the questions and affirmations on the back side of the sheet). Allow your energy to shift as you begin working this side.

---

8. I now realize that (X) and I have both been receiving exactly what we each had subconsciously chosen: *(Comment on this).*

I realize that subconsciously I wanted to be treated as if I wasn't enough, so that my belief around that would be forced to come to the surface. Only then would I be able to heal it and let it go. My higher Self knew what I had to do. Jeff's Higher Self knew too - and I recognize that there was a healing in there somewhere for him too - so we both benefitted at some level. We both needed this experience in order to grow.

---

8. This serves as yet another reminder of the Law of Cause and Effect and of how we can instantly become aware of our subconscious beliefs if we look at what we have in our lives from this viewpoint. Our ability to create our lives through the Law of Cause and Effect, means that *what we have* at any particular point in time truly *is what we want*. We have, at the soul level, chosen our situations and experiences, and our choices are not wrong.

Creating difficulties in our lives does not make us spiritual cripples, for these difficulties teach us what we need to learn. Our Higher Self (soul) creates these circumstances so we can transform the beliefs, patterns and feelings inherent in the difficulties. Remember that transformation begins with accepting these beliefs, patterns and feelings and in loving them. Loving the people who mirror these beliefs, patterns and feelings for us creates the same effect.

So look at your situation, and see it as perfect feedback. Then bless X for co-creating with you the situation so you could become aware of the beliefs that create your life. After all, X deserves your gratitude and blessings since this co-creation and subsequent awareness gives you the ability to know your beliefs, which, in turn, empowers you with the ability to let them go. When you do so, you can make another choice immediately about your beliefs and what you want to create in your life.

> **9. LETTING GO**
>
> I release from my consciousness all **feelings of:** *(as in 2b)*
>
> *Hurt, abandonment, betrayal, sadness and anger.*
>
> I release from my consciousness all **thoughts of:** *(as in 2c)*
>
> *You having betrayed me, hurt me and wanting to make me feel worthless.*

9. In Step #2, you stated your thoughts truthfully and owned your feelings, thus allowing yourself to feel your emotions without any judgment whatsoever. Now comes the time to let them move through you and be released. As long as these emotions and thoughts remain in your consciousness, they block your awareness of the misperception that is causing the upset. If you still feel strongly about the situation, you still have an investment in whatever the misperception is -- your belief, interpretation, judgment, etc. Do not judge this fact or try to change your investment. Just notice it.

Your emotions about your situation may come back time and time again, and you can make that okay, too. Just be willing to feel them and then release them -- at least for the moment — so the light of awareness can shine through you and allow you to see the misperception. Then, once again, you can choose to see the situation differently.

Releasing emotions and corresponding thoughts serves an important role in the forgiveness process. As long as those thoughts remain operative, they continue lending energy to our old belief systems, which created the reality we now are trying to transform. Affirming that we release both the feeling and the thoughts attached to them begins the healing process.

> I completely forgive you (X)   *Jeff.*
> for I now realize that you did nothing to me and I drop my Ego's demand that you cater to all my dependency needs and become my scapegoat. **I acknowledge, accept and love you unconditionally just the way you are.**

• The first part of this statement provides further evidence of your willingness to accept responsibility for what happens to you and to release the need to play the victim role. By taking this first step in the forgiveness process, you recognize that what you attack and judge in others represents what you condemn in yourself.

When you stop demanding that X be a certain way, you free X and yourself from the tyranny of a co-dependent relationship and from the unconscious agreement to support each other in your misperceptions, as well as to be the willing scapegoats for each other. This agreement keeps you stuck in the illusion and in victim consciousness. Therefore, it must go!

As you *acknowledge, accept and love X unconditionally just the way he or she is,* you recognize and forgive the projection that made you see X as less than perfect. You can love X without judgment now, because you realize that is the only way a person can be loved. You can

love X now, because you realize that how he/she appears
in the world represents the only way he or she can be.
That is how Spirit has willed him or her to be for you.

---

10. I now realize that what I was experiencing was a precise reflection of how I perceived the situation. I understand that I can
change the experience by changing the perception. I have released
my attachment to that original perception and am willing to see it
differently. *(Attempt a new perception).*

*I now see that Jeff was simply mirroring my false
belief that I was unloveable and he was giving me
the gift of healing. Jeff loves me so much, he was
willing to endure the discomfort of acting it out
for me. Bless you, Jeff. I now realize that I am
responsible for healing the situation for myself
and I thank you for doing this for me.*

---

10. If you look back at section #1 on the worksheet, you
may find that, as a result of the work you have done on the
worksheet, your energy has changed sufficiently for you to
entertain another interpretation of the situation — an interpretation based on principles of Radical Forgiveness.

*Note: It is not helpful to create a new interpretation or
your situation based on assumptions rooted in the World
of Humanity. Such an interpretation might involve giving an explanation for the situation or making some*

kind of an excuse for X's behavior. As we saw in Chapter 2, this comes over more as pseudo forgiveness; it moves little energy and certainly does not undo your projection. Unless your projection changes, nothing else will change.

A new interpretation of your situation should make you feel its perfection and be open to the gift it offers you. Seek a way of looking at your situation that reveals the hand of God or Divine Intelligence working for you and showing you how much it loves you.

Look for the opportunity to join with X (and anyone else involved in your situation) by realizing that what you have perceived as a threat or an attack from X really was a cry for love. Also realize that this cry for love exactly mirrored your own cry for love. A shift in perception such as this represents what we call a "miracle."

Note: It may take completing many worksheets on the same issue to get to this new perception. Be absolutely truthful with yourself, and always work from your feelings. There are no right answers, no goals, no grades, and no end products here. The value lies in the process, in doing the work. Let whatever comes be perfect, and resist the urge to edit and evaluate what you write. When you have moved into a feeling of unconditional love for X, you will know you have resolved your issue and have no need to do more worksheets.

11. I completely forgive myself *Jill*
and accept myself as a loving, generous, creative being. I release all
need to hold onto negative emotions and ideas of lack and limitations. I withdraw my energy from the past and release all barriers
against the love and abundance that I know I have already. I create
my thoughts, my feelings and my life and I am empowered to be
myself again, to unconditionally love and support myself, just the
way I am, in all my magnificence.

11. The importance of this affirmation cannot be overem-
phasized. Say it out loud, and let yourself feel it. Let the
words resonate within you. Self-judgment resides at the
root of all our problems, and even when we have removed
judgment from others and forgiven them, we continue to
judge ourselves. We even judge ourselves for judging ourselves!

The difficulty we experience in trying to break this cycle
results from the fact that the Ego's survival depends on us
feeling guilty about who we are. The more successfully we
forgive others, the more the Ego tries to compensate by
making us feel guilty about ourselves. This explains why
we can expect to encounter enormous resistance to moving through the forgiveness process. The Ego feels threat-
ened at every step, and *it will* put up a fight. We see the
results of this internal struggle when we do not complete a
Forgiveness Worksheet, when we create more reasons to
continue projection onto X and feeling victimized, when
we do not find time to meditate or forget to do other things
that support us in remembering who we are. The closer
we get to letting go of something that elicits the feeling of

guilt the more the Ego kicks and screams, thus the more difficult the forgiveness process seems.

Be willing to go through the resistance, knowing that on the other side lies peace and joy. Be willing also to feel any pain, depression, chaos and confusion that might occur while you are going through it.

> **12.** I now SURRENDER to the Higher Power that I know as _God_ and trust in the knowledge that this situation will continue to unfold perfectly and in accordance with Divine guidance.
>
> I acknowledge my Oneness and feel my myself totally re-connected with my Source. I am restored to my true nature which is LOVE and restore love to (X) _Jeff_

12. This represents the final step in the forgiveness process. However, it is *not* your step to take. You affirm that you are willing to experience it and turn the remainder of the process over to the Higher Power. Ask that healing be completed by Divine grace and that you and X be joined. In joining, you both return to wholeness and love by connecting to your Source.

> I close my eyes in order to feel the Love that flows in my life and to feel the joy that comes when the Love is felt and expressed.

• You have had the opportunity to see the inherent perfection in your situation and to redefine the situation in terms of Divine Truth. Though it works best to do this at the feeling level, sometimes we have no choice but to work through the process verbally and through the written word as we have done here. However, this final step offers you the opportunity to drop the words, the thoughts and the concepts and to actually *feel* the love. When you reach the bottom line, only love exists. If you can truly tap into that love, you are home free. You need do nothing else.

So, take a few minutes to meditate on this statement, and be open to feeling the love. You may have to try this exercise many times before you feel it, but one day, just when you least expect it, the love will envelop you. Then, you will feel the joy as well.

---

13. A Note To You (X)   "Having done this worksheet today, I.....

I realize how lucky I am to have you in my life.

I knew we were meant to be together for a reason and now I know what it was.

---

13. You began the Forgiveness Worksheet by confronting X. Your energy probably has shifted since you began, even if the shift occurred only a moment or two ago. How do you feel about X now? What would you like to say to X? Allow yourself to write without conscious thought, if possible, and do not judge your words. Let them surprise even you.

14. A Note To Myself

I honor myself for having the courage to go through this and for being able to get beyond being the victim - I am FREE!

14. Remember, all forgiveness starts as a lie. You begin the process without forgiveness in your heart, and *you fake it until you make it.* So, be gentle with yourself, and let the forgiveness process take as long as you need. Be patient with yourself. Acknowledge yourself for the courage it takes simply to attempt completing the Forgiveness Worksheet, for you truly face your demons in the process. Doing this work takes enormous courage, willingness and faith. Honor yourself for doing it.

30: A Radical Forgiveness Reframe

We have learned to judge the circumstances of our lives according to a relatively stable framework of ideas, concepts and beliefs about life, about the world and our place within the world. We literally frame all our experiences with them. For example:

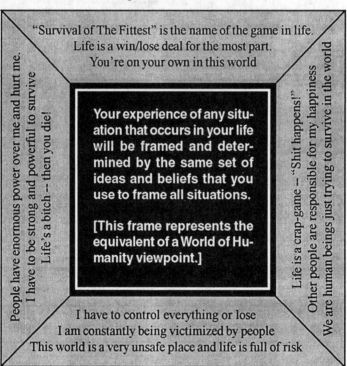

"Survival of The Fittest" is the name of the game in life.
Life is a win/lose deal for the most part.
You're on your own in this world

People have enormous power over me and hurt me.
I have to be strong and powerful to survive
Life's a bitch -- then you die!

Your experience of any situation that occurs in your life will be framed and determined by the same set of ideas and beliefs that you use to frame all situations.

[This frame represents the equivalent of a World of Humanity viewpoint.]

Life is a crap-game -- "Shit happens!"
Other people are responsible for my happiness
We are human beings just trying to survive in the world

I have to control everything or lose
I am constantly being victimized by people
This world is a very unsafe place and life is full of risk

With a Radical Forgiveness Reframe, in our mind or in actuality, we symbolically replace the existing frame with one consisting of Radical Forgiveness principles. Like doing the worksheet, this opens our minds to a new interpretation of the situation and allows a shift in perception as to its meaning.

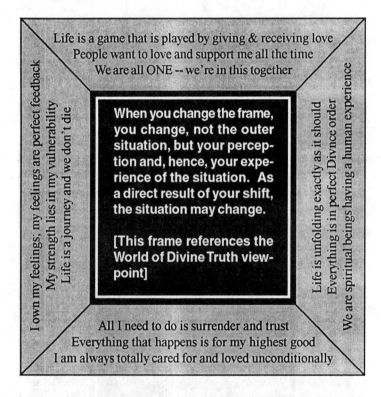

Life is a game that is played by giving & receiving love
People want to love and support me all the time
We are all ONE -- we're in this together

I own my feelings; my feelings are perfect feedback
My strength lies in my vulnerability
Life is a journey and we don't die

Life is unfolding exactly as it should
Everything is in perfect Divnce order
We are spiritual beings having a human experience

When you change the frame, you change, not the outer situation, but your perception and, hence, your experience of the situation. As a direct result of your shift, the situation may change.

[This frame references the World of Divine Truth viewpoint]

All I need to do is surrender and trust
Everything that happens is for my highest good
I am always totally cared for and loved unconditionally

First journal the situation you need to forgive, or transend, just as you see it and then do the Radical Forgiveness Reframe by mentally framing what you have written with these statements, taking time to meditate on each statement. Then attempt another interpretation.

Epilogue: Goodbye England's Rose

I began this book with a story about my sister Jill. The purpose of it was to illustrate how a seemingly desperate situation can be transformed when we approach it from the standpoint of Radical Forgiveness.

Just a few days before going to print, fate handed me an opportunity to end the book with a story that was equally instructive and open to a Radical Forgiveness perspective.

Unlike the one about Jill, this story was one with which virtually everyone in the world was familiar, as well as deeply involved emotionally. I refer of course to the story of Princess Diana who made her unexpected transition in the early hours of Sunday, August 31, 1997.

The drama began for me when my lifetime friend, Peter Jollyman, woke me with a phone call from England. For him it was around midday, but for me in Atlanta, it was still early and I had not yet seen a newspaper or listened to the radio. "Have you heard about the accident?" he asked. "What accident?" I replied, still in a stupor but aware enough to realize this had to be serious for him to be calling like this. "Princess Di was killed last night in a car crash in Paris. She was being chased by paparazzi. Her car spun out of control and hit a concrete post. She and Dodi were killed."

I noticed a perfunctory pang of remorse pass through me as I listened to the details as best he knew them at the time, but I can't say that it lasted more than a few moments. I tried to sound suitably shocked, but I really felt somewhat ambivalent about it.

Lot's of people died in the last 24 hours, I thought, after I put the phone down. Why would her death be any more, or any less, tragic than anyone else's. It was her time to go and that's about all there is to it. Sad for her two boys though, of course. With that, I went downstairs to make tea and fix breakfast.

Then I turned on the TV and from that moment on, slowly began to get drawn into, and involved with, what was to become, in the days culminating in her funeral on Saturday morning, a roller-coaster of emotion. As the days went by, I realized that something quite extraordinary was going on. The reaction to Princess Diana's death, not only in England, but throughout the world, was truly phenomenal. As I saw my countrymen on the TV in heartfelt pain, crying and grieving in public — something English people simply do not do ordinarily — I found myself feeling the same emotions and crying with them. I was shocked to realize that I was hurting too. Somehow this woman, whom I had never met or thought much about, especially during the thirteen years I have lived in the U.S., had touched me deeply. I felt the loss profoundly and I was very surprised.

I really began to pay attention and to wonder what was really happening here. Something of extraordinarily deep significance was occurring and I began an inner search to find the message and the meaning in it. Diana's death clearly had meaning far beyond the apparent circumstances in which it occurred, dramatic as they appeared to be. Some higher purpose was being played out here.

Then on Wednesday, it hit me. As I watched the scenes from England and experienced the great outpouring of emotion from people not in the least renowned for showing their emotions, especially in the open, I suddenly realized what Diana's spiritual mission had been. The over-arching purpose of her incarnation had been to open the heart chakra of Great Britain and by so doing, greatly accelerate the spiritual evolution of the British people, no less. I had no doubt whatsoever that she had achieved exactly that.

No one who watched the events of that week could ever doubt that she had single-handedly transformed the country — and indeed, much of the world — at the heart level. Only a very few people in all of human history come to mind as having had such an effect on the world purely through the expression of love energy. Ghandi, Martin Luther-King and Nelson Mandela perhaps; Mother Teresa and Jesus Christ, certainly. *(No wonder the Queen of England bowed her head to Diana's coffin — something never before witnessed.)*

While in terms of human achievement and spiritual example in life, any comparison with Mother Teresa would be unfair, it is nevertheless interesting to note that the death of

253

Mother Teresa, whose life and work, in most people's eyes, has brought her close to sainthood in her lifetime, did not take the spotlight off Diana even for a moment. That two women whose lives so deeply touched the world through authentic love should make their transitions within days of each other like this has enormous spiritual significance.

Even though the British people had been through two wars this century, suffering and grieving enormous losses, they came through it all with their legendary sense of humor and proverbial stiff upper lip, but not, I think it is fair to say, with an open heart. That had to wait, not only the coming of a people's princess, but her divinely planned and, to us at least, untimely and tragic death.

Since then, commentators have tried in vain to explain her effect on the world in terms of our fixation on, and willingness to almost deify, celebrities we know only through the media. Jonathan Alter in Newsweek came closer than most be referring to what Richard Sennett, in *The Fall of Public Man*, called the ideology of intimacy, in which people "seek to find personal meaning in impersonal situations." It is true that people did not know her personally and to that extent it remains an impersonal situation. Yet she transcended those limitations imposed by time and space and somehow touched everyone's heart very deeply in a way that cannot be easily explained.

The key to understanding her power as a human being lies in the archetype of the wounded healer, which teaches us that our power lies in our wounds — in the sense that it is the wound in me that evokes the healing in you and the wound in you that evokes the healing in me. We are all wounded healers but we don't know it. When we keep our wounds hidden and totally private, we separate from, and deny healing, not only to ourselves, but to countless others too. The stiff upper lip is a terrible way to withhold love. It atrophies the heart and cripples the soul. Through her willingness to share her deepest wounds with the whole world, Princess Diana evoked the healer in all of us, opened our hearts and healed our fractured souls.

The whole world watched as people took their cue from Diana and opened up, sharing their grief and their woundedness, just as she had done. She gave the people a language of intimacy that they could use to express feelings openly and authentically. I don't recall seeing one display of emotion and feeling that was not totally authentic, and on television today that is indeed unusual.

As we each begin to emerge from behind the pain of loss and the rope burns of grief, anger and projection of guilt regarding our insatiable appetite for Diana's image and curiosity about her life, which the press and papparazzi merely reflected for us, we begin to discern, through the mists and veils, the divine perfection of it all. The more we contemplate the mission she accepted and the extent to which she succeeded, the more we are able to surrender into that perfection.

We find ourselves experiencing a new level of peace as we move beyond the emotions and thoughts that once would have tied us to the World of Humanity forever and held us hostage to the victim archetype, towards the acceptance of the fact that it all had to unfold in exactly that way. The mission absolutely required the upbringing that she had, the marriage that went terribly wrong, the rejection she suffered at the hands of the royal establishment, the criticism of the press, the hounding by the paparazzi, the dramatic and violent death — everything, down to the very last detail.

And as the future unfolds, you will notice that now Diana has returned 'home' having completed her mission, the energies that held all those dynamics in place will begin to disperse. Not only is she released from those dynamics, so are all the other people who were involved in the drama we know to be only an illusion. Charles is now free to become warmer, less distant and a more loving father to his two boys — and he undoubtedly will. (The Press will say that he changed because of what happened, but we will know the real truth.) The Queen will probably become less stuffy, more open and not quite so irrelevant. The monarchy itself will transcend the cult of personality and will become a stronger, more meaningful institution, not as a direct response to what happened, but because of the energy shift that occurred when the mission was over and the transformation complete.

But just because someone opens their heart chakra, there's no guarantee that they will keep it open. That remains a matter of choice at every moment. The same is true of the collective. The British people, and others around the world, will either stay in the love vibration that Diana's death cata-pulted them into, and use that power to transform them-selves, their royal family and their society, or they will fo-cus on the illusion of what happened, blaming Charles, the royal family in general, the driver, the press and others. If they choose the latter, that will be their choice and perfect in its own way, but it will cause the collective heart chakra to close again.

Perhaps this book has a part to play in keeping the collec-tive heart chakra open. Maybe the insight you have gained by reading it will enable you to remain focussed, not on the illusion of what happened in the tunnel that night in Paris, but on what is real in the Princess Diana story from begin-ning to end and the mission that gave it meaning and sig-nificance.

Maybe everyone who reads this book will truly recognize and acknowledge that, just as Jeff played his part for Jill in the story of Part one, Charles played his part beautifully for Diana — as did Camilla Parker-Bowles and the Queen. Maybe it will be clear to everyone who reads this book that the drama called for such loving, courageous souls to play those parts in exactly those ways and, let it be said, at great cost to themselves. (Charles' sacrifice for the sake of the opening of the heart chakra of Britain was abso-lutely no less than Diana's — in fact, in ordinary human terms, probably greater. It may have cost him his crown, no less!)

Maybe too, it will be obvious to everyone that it was all agreed up-front, prior to each character's souls incarnating into this world and that the paparazzi were also playing an essential and loving part in all this too, as were the editors who paid for intrusive pictures of Diana.

Those who are indeed able to do the Radical Forgiveness reframe to this extent, recognizing that there were no victims here, will be a great beacon of light to all those who might otherwise choose to focus on the illusion, close their hearts and lose the love vibration. It is my fervent hope that every reader who is changed by my book will become a beacon of love — taking over where Diana left off, helping people stay in this new and higher vibration that her perfectly timed transition triggered.

And it seems to me that you lived your life
like a candle in the wind:
never fading with the sunset
when the rain came in.
And your footsteps will always fall here,
along England's greenest hills;
your candle's burned out long before
your legend ever will.

From © "Candle in the Wind," Polygram International, Inc. Written and performed by Elton John in Westminster Abbey at the funeral of Diana, Princess of Wales, September 6, 1997.

Appendix I

Training and Certification in RFT

Our vision is to train many thousands of people who will be able to articulate the principles of Radical Forgiveness to others in a simple and clear way, in order that more and more people have the opportunity to raise their vibration and shift their consciousness towards an alignment with spiritual principle. We see this as supporting the mission that we have accepted for ourselves, which is to *raise the consciousness of the planet through the message of Radical Forgiveness.*

We envision therapists of all kinds integrating RFT into their work. We also see ordinary people, having trained with us, hosting Radical Forgiveness healing groups, or support groups, in their homes on a regular basis as well as having conversations one-on-one with people who might benefit from being exposed to these ideas.

The training is for anyone who feels drawn towards this work and desires the training experience. Level One Training (which is an open workshop that anyone can attend, either for their own healing or as the first level of training, or both), is the only prerequisite for Level Two. However, the training is ideal for those with existing expertise and qualifications in psychotherapy, counseling, hypnotherapy, pastoral care, mind/body/spirit healing, or spiritual coaching. *See our announcement on the back page*).

Please note, we are not offering basic training for therapists. Our intention is to give professionals another tool to add to their own repertoire of techniques, while at the same time training people who are non-therapists how to educate and coach others in Radical Forgiveness so that they too can spread the word and have an effect on the world.

Graduates will be able to use the Radical Forgiveness Therapy (RFT) logo/trademark in all their advertising and promotion and will be listed as registered RFT practitioners, or coaches, in a national and international RFT database and referral network.

The training totals 70 hours of experiential study, taking place over three weekends. An alternative arrangement is two weekends plus a written 10,000 word thesis or clinical report. Training is normally based in Atlanta, though local trainings in your area can be set up by arrangement.

Further information can be obtained from our Web site at *www.radicalforgiveness.com,* or by calling 1-888-755-5696 or by writing to The Radical Forgiveness Therapy Center, PO Box 440572, Kennesaw, GA 30144, U.S.A.

Appendix II

Worksheet Masters

The forgiveness worksheets provided here were designed to be printed on 8.5" X 11" paper, but have been reduced to 60% of their full size to fit the book. Any good photocopy shop will restore them to full-size for you.

Making Room for the Miracle is two sided, while Miracles is one sided.

A preferred solution is to order from us some pristine copies of these worksheets (plus the Release Letter), laminated in heavy duty plastic for long term use. With these as your masters you won't find yourself making copies from copies and getting to the point where the quality is so bad you won't be able to read the print. For ordering information, see the order form in Appendix V.

Making Room for The Miracle

A Radical Forgiveness Worksheet

Date: ▨▨▨▨ Worksheet # ▨▨▨▨   Subject: (X) *Whomever or whatever you are upset about:* ▨▨▨▨▨▨

1. The situation as I perceive it now is:

BREATHE

Confronting Subject (X)

2a) I am upset because:

2b) I am feeling: *(Identify your real emotions here).*

2c) I think: *(Identify the thoughts attached to the emotions).*

3. I lovingly recognize and accept my feelings, *(as in 2b)* without judgment, of:

I own my feelings. No-one can make me feel anything. My feelings are a reflection of my consciousness around the situation.

4. Even though I do not know why, I recognize that I have created this situation in order that I can learn and grow. *(Comment on this and attempt a possible explanation for why you may have created the situation).*

5. FIVE INSIGHTS IN RADICAL FORGIVENESS: AFFIRM NOW.

a. When I feel uncomfortable, I know there is a part of me that needs to be healed. (X) ▨▨▨▨▨▨ is reflecting this for me so that I can see what I need to forgive in myself.

b. I now realize that I get upset only when someone resonates in me what I have denied, repressed and projected onto others. The situation is a precise mirror of my consciousness around this issue.

c. I now realize that the way I see (X) is precisely the way I unconsciously see myself. In forgiving (X), I forgive myself.

d. I appreciate your willingness (x) ▨▨▨▨▨▨ to mirror my misperceptions, and I bless you for providing me with the opportunity to practice Radical Forgiveness and heal.

e. I now see that I am a spiritual being having a human experience, and I forgive my Ego for using guilt, anger, blame and judgment to lower my vibration and keep me separated from the World of DivineTruth.

6. I now realize that nothing (X), or anyone else, has done is either right or wrong. I drop all judgment. I release the need to blame and the need to be right and I recognize the perfection in the situation just the way it is. *(Comment truthfully on this.)*

7. My discomfort was my signal that I was witholding love from myself and others. *(Describe how you were witholding love)*

Acknowledgements: Dr. Michael Ryce and Arnold M. Patent.

8. I now realize that (X) and I have both been receiving exactly what we each had subconsciously chosen: *(Comment on this).*

9. **LETTING GO:**

I release from my consciousness all feelings of: *(as in 2b)*

I release from my consciousness all thoughts of: (as in 2C)

I completely forgive you (x) ▨▨▨▨▨▨▨ for I now realize that you did nothing to me and I drop my Ego's demand that you cater to all my dependency needs and become my scapegoat. I acknowledge, accept and love you unconditionally just the way you are.

10. I now realize that what I was experiencing was a precise reflection of how I perceived the situation. I understand that I can change the experience by changing the perception. I have released my attachment to that original perception and am willing to see it differently now. *(Attempt a new perception - this may or may not be the same as in box #4)*

11. I completely forgive myself, ▨▨▨▨▨▨▨ and accept myself as a loving, generous and creative being. I release all need to hold onto emotions and ideas of lack and limitation connected to the past. I withdraw my energy from the past and release all barriers against the love and abundance that I know I have in this moment. I create my life and I am empowered to be myself again, to unconditionally love and support myself, just the way I am, in all my power and magnificence.

12. I now SURRENDER to the Higher Power I think of as

▨▨▨▨▨▨▨

and trust in the knowledge that this situation will continue to unfold perfectly and in accordance with Divine guidance and spiritual law.

I acknowledge my Oneness and feel myself totally reconnected with my Source. I am restored to my true nature, which is LOVE, and I now restore love to (X) ▨▨▨▨▨▨

I close my eyes in order to feel the LOVE that flows in my life and to feel the joy that comes when the love is felt and expressed.

13. A Note To You (X)   Having done this worksheet, I.........

14. A Note To Myself:

Acknowledgements: Dr. Michael Ryce and Arnold M. Patent.

"Miracles" FORGIVENESS WORKSHEET

Date: ▨▨▨▨ Worksheet # ▨▨▨▨ Subject: (X) *Whomever or whatever you are upset about:* ▨▨▨▨▨▨▨

1. The situation as I perceive it now is:

BREATHE

Confronting Subject (X)

2. I am upset because....

BREATHE

3. I lovingly recognize and accept my feelings, without judgment, of:

I own my feeling. No-one can make me feel anything. I recognize that I have chosen to have these feeling and that's OK because these feeling are ME. I love the feelings because they are ME, and I love myself for having the feelings because my life energy IS my feelings.   WHEN I AM FEELING - IAM ALIVE!

4. I choose to now open my heart and flow forgiveness to (X)

I release the blame, judgment and guilt I have held onto for so long, for I no longer wish to carry that load. I BRING MY ENERGY BACK INTO PRESENT TIME IN ORDER TO HEAL AND GROW.

5. As I flow forgiveness to (X) ▨▨▨▨ **, I recognize that** he/ she/ it was reflecting a part of me that needs to be healed. I now realize that I only get upset when someone resonates in me what I have denied, repressed and projected onto others. In forgiving this person, I forgive myself and heal myself. I am grateful to this person for helping me HEAL AND GROW, for helping me FULFILL MY MISSION and supporting me in my SPIRITUAL GROWTH.

6. As I flow forgiveness to (X) ▨▨▨▨ **I re-**lease all blame and judgment - and the need to be right. As a result, I notice my feelings have changed. I now feel........

7. As I flow forgiveness to (X) ▨▨▨▨ **I am now able** to see the situation differently. For example:

8. What I would like to say now to (X) ▨▨▨▨ **is:**

9. A note to myself:

Acknowledgements: Dr. Michael Ryce, Arnold M. Patent, Caroline Myss and 'Abraham.'

Appendix III

Many workshop attendees request these recipes:

1. Mock Turtle Soup

1/4 cup light oil
1/2 stick butter
1/4 lb. beef finely cubed
1/4 lb. chopped pork
1/4 lb. chopped chicken
5 cups brown stock
1/3 cup All Purpose flour
2 med onions finely diced
2 ribs of celery finely diced
1/2 green pepper finely diced
1/2 red pepper finely diced

1/2 cup green scallions
1/4 cup tomato puree
1/4 cup fresh parsely
1/2 teaspoon dried thyme
Louisiana Hot sauce, Tobasco
or cayenne pepper & salt.
Juice of one lemon
Lemon slices
Sherry
2 hard-boiled eggs finely diced
(OR) 4 Mock Turtle Eggs.

Brown the meat thoroughly in the oil and butter, then remove and set aside. Add the flour and make a dark roux. (This means gently cooking the flour in the oil, stirring frequently, until it eventually becomes a rich dark brown color. This may take 45 minutes, so it requires some patience. You can be working in between stirs — and its worth the extra effort in the taste. Do not burn!) The, add the onions, celery, peppers, parsely, and thyme, stirring continuously. Cook until onions are clear. Then add 1 cup of stock to make a thick paste, and add the tomato puree. Slowly add the remaining stock plus the meat, hot sauce and salt. Simmer for two hours stirring occasionally and then add the chopped egg and simmer for a further half hour. (If using the mock turtle eggs, drop them in just before serving.) Add scallions just before serving and cook for two minutes. Garnish with a lemon slice and a few chopped scallions and add a dash of sherry. Serves four.

For the vegetarian version, either replace the meats with a smooth puree of red beans or, if you prefer a meat-like texture, use a vegetarian meat substitute. You can get them cubed and they saute just like meat.

2. Mock Turtle Eggs

3 hardboiled eggs
1 raw egg
1 level tablespoon of all-purpose flour
Salt, pepper and cayenne pepper to taste.

Bring a saucepan of water to a boil. Have it boiling while you blend the eggs, flour and seasoning in a blender or food processor until smooth. Roll and form into small eggs, and roll them in flour. Drop them into the boiling water and boil for 3 minutes. These can be done ahead of time and stored in a tight container in the refrigerator.

This adds a little more effort to the process of making this delicious soup, but it adds a whole new dimension to the gastronomical experience.

Appendix IV

Turtle Soup For The Soul

Almost everyone has, or soon will have, I hope, a forgiveness story to tell. *I would like to give you the opportunity to share yours with me and possibly to have it included in future books of mine.*

When Jack Canfield and Mark Victor Hanson wrote "Chicken Soup for the Soul" *(Health Communications, Inc. 1993),* they proved that people are hungry for stories that feed their soul — especially inspirational stories written by ordinary people like themselves.

Do not let your belief about your writing skill deter you from sending me your forgiveness story. I want to read the story in your own words, grammatically correct or not, misspelled or not. Our editors will take care of all that — it's your story that's important!

All stories submitted should be relatively brief, long enough to tell the story but not too long. Do not take my story about Jill as a model. I used that as a teaching device. If I were writing Jill's story to submit here, I would do it in two or three pages. Anyway, story-telling is always more powerful for being concise.

The story you send need not be limited to your own experience. You may know others who have an inspiring story to tell. However, you should ask them if they would like to submit their own story or, if not, whether they would allow you to submit it on their behalf. I insist, however, on knowing the source of any story and always reserve the right to talk with that individual directly, even if they did not actually send the story themselves. We cannot accept hearsay or apocryphal stories.

I am also planning a book on *Rituals and Ceremonies For Healing and Forgiveness,* so I would also like to receive your suggestions for any rituals and ceremonies that you have found to be powerful and effective for healing and forgiveness — or that could be adapted for that purpose. I will acknowledge the source of anything I publish and all writers will be compensated for their work.

It is very important that you send it to me by E-mail. That way I can bring it into my computer and work on it directly. The E-mail address is *stories@radicalforgiveness.com.*

Failing that, mail it to me on a diskette (IBM compatible), to P.O. Box 440572, Kennesaw, GA 30411. Only if your story is very short, less than one typed page, should you mail it to me as hard copy or fax it to (770) 429-0276.

I am very excited about this and really encourage you to send in your stories and suggestions. I look forward to hearing from you.

Appendix V

Additional Resource Materials

This appendix gives a brief description of a selection of additional resources available from Colin Tipping through The Radical Forgiveness Therapy Center. An order form is included at the back of the book.

• **This Book On Audio Tape**
  (scheduled for Spring '99)

  (Item #2 on the order form).

• **Plastic Laminated Masters of Worksheets**

  Combination Pack of 8.5" X 11" Durable,
  Two Sided Masters of:
  'Making Room for the Miracle,' worksheet.
  'Miracles' worksheet & 'Radical Release Letter.'

  (Item #5 on the order form).

• Audio Tapes

1. Radical Forgiveness Meditations
Side A: The Rose Forgiveness Meditation
Side B: A Wake For Your Wounded Inner Child

Professionally recorded renditions by the author of
the Radical Forgiveness meditations that appear in
Part 4 of this book.   **(Item # 6 on the order form).**

2. Making Room for the Miracle
Side A: The Essence of Radical Forgiveness
Side B: How to use the 'Miracles' worksheet

This tape outlines the essential principles of, and the
spiritual assumptions underlying, the theory and the
practice of Radical Forgiveness. On side two, you are
provided careful coaching on how the use some forgiveness tools; in particular the **'Miracles'** worksheet.
This one is a little different from the "Making Room for
the Miracle," worksheet featured in detail in the book.
You will find a copy of 'Miracles' in the previous appendix and a laminated version in the pack for sale here.

*This tape may be a life-line for you in moments of
crisis. Play it as a reminder that, no matter how
things look, you are exactly where you need to be
and everything is in Divine order.*

                    (Item #7 on the order form.)

• The "ARTFUL Transformations"
Forgiveness Coloring Meditation Kit

A tool that takes you through a powerful 90 minute art-therapy based forgiveness process for the inner child and the wounded adult. Kit includes paper, crayons, instructions and a meditation tape.

This specially prepared meditation bypasses the normal verbal barriers to the subconscious mind and gets the results you want. The process is similar to writing the 'trilogy of letters' as outlined in Chapter 23 of this book, but here we guide you through the intuitive production of a series of "visually explicit, uncensored emotional statements" on paper, that come from deep within yourself. Absolutely NO artistic talent whatsoever is required. **(Item #3 on the order form).**

• *The Essence of Radical Forgiveness*

This book serves both as an introduction to Radical Forgiveness and a quick reference reminder of the principles and processes. Ideal as a gift, it contains *'Jill's Story,'* as well as an outline of the basic assumptions of Radical Forgiveness, the 4-Step Forgiveness process and instructions on how to use the "Miracles" forgiveness worksheet.

(Item #4 on the order form).

ORDER FORM

Please rush me the following items

# Qty:	Item:		
1. ☐	Book: Radical Forgiveness @ 16.95	$	_____
2. ☐	Audio Book: R.F. @ $16.95	$	_____
3. ☐	The Artful Transformation Kit @ 21.95	$	_____
4. ☐	The Essence of R.F. (Gift book) @ $7.50	$	_____
5. ☐	Combo pack Laminated Masters @ $10.00	$	_____
6. ☐	Audio Tape "RF" Meditations @ $10.00	$	_____
7. ☐	Audio Tape "Making Room" @ $10.00	$	_____

Sub Total $_____

GA Residents add sales tax appropriate to county

of residence: County _____ Rate ____ $_____

Shipping & Handling. Add $2.50 for #1 & 2;

$3.50 for #3; $2.00 for #4,5, 6 & 7. $_____

Total Amount For the Order | $ |

Telephone Orders: **1-888-755-5696** FAX Orders **770-429-0276**
E-mail Orders: *sales@radicalforgiveness.com*
Mail Orders: RF Center, PO Box 440572, Kennesaw, GA 30144.

Name:_____

Address: _____

City:_____ State: __Zip: _____

Payment: Check Money Order   Visa/MC

Card # _____Expires._____

Appendix VI

Workshops, Seminars & Lectures
By Colin Tipping

Colin Tipping is an international speaker and regulary conducts lectures, seminars and workshops in Radical Forgiveness and related health issues. He also trains and certifies people in his own Radical Forgiveness Therapy.

He is a founder/director of Together-We-Heal, Inc., a nonprofit corporation dedicated to emotional and spiritual healing and, with his wife JoAnna has, for more than six years, run 5-day healing retreats for people with cancer in the U.S., and U.K., as well as other intensive healing retreats for people interested in a holistic mind/body approach to getting well.

Colin is currently based in Atlanta and he conducts most of his weekend workshops and training workshops for certification in Radical Forgiveness Therapy in that area. However, he is increasingly being booked to speak in other cities in the U.S. and overseas.

For an up to date workshop schedule, refer to his web site; **www.radicalforgiveness.com.** or call **1-888-755-5696**

• Introductory Seminars and Lectures:

These are typically 2 -3 hours in length and are designed as an introduction to the ideas, underlying assumptions and concepts of Radical Forgiveness. A Unity church is a typical venue for such an event.

• One-day Workshops:

These workshops are more intensive in character than the seminars and involve experiential work in Radical Forgiveness as well as the more exploratory conceptual work. It is not expected that the attendees shall necessarily have read the book, though it is an advantage.

• Weekend Workshops

These workshops are for people who have read this book or are familiar with the concepts, and want some 'hands-on' assistance and gentle guidance from Colin, in a safe and loving workshop environment, in moving through their own forgiveness issues. This is a practical and experiential workshop which is almost invariably life-changing for those who attend.

• 5-day or 10-day Healing Intensives

These residential healing retreats, co-facilitated with Donna Gates, author of "The Body Ecology Diet," are for people who need support in *getting well*. The approach is holistic and multi-faceted and includes Satori Breathwork, bodywork, dietary support and cleansing combined with emotional and spiritual work based on the Radical Forgiveness approach.

• *Custom Designed Workshops For Business*

The application of Radical Forgiveness principles to any business organization will almost certainly increase productivity, raise morale, improve customer relations and boost the bottom line. As soon as people realize that difficult relationship situations at work are simply opportunities to heal, all barriers come down. Hearts then open and a whole new way of relating to each other, to customers and to the company itself, is created. Our workshops, appropriate for any level, enable people to work more in spiritual alignment with each other and in support of mutual goals and aspirations. The effects can be dramatic, long lasting and profound.

• *A Retreat For Top Management*

Tracking the *'energy'* in an organization, analysing where it flows best and where it is blocked, and then redirecting it so it aligns more closely with the company's mission, is the purpose of this workshop. Since *energy analysis* is always a top-down process, the retreat is designed specifically for a company's top management team. Radical Forgiveness processes are then used to free blocked energy in the system so that more creativity, productivity, trust, synergy and common purpose within the organization can flourish. The effects that this can have on a company, especially if workshops are offered at lower levels too, are potentially very rewarding.

Call Colin Tipping, at the Radical Forgiveness Therapy Center, to discuss your needs for corporate workshops and executive training retreats. (1-888-755-5696)